General Editor:

Media Sociology

David Barrat

MEDIA SOCIOLOGY

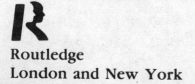

Routledge
London and New York

First published 1986 by
Tavistock Publications Ltd

Reprinted 1990
by Routledge
11 New Fetter Lane,
London EC4P 4EE

29 West 35th Street,
New York, NY 10001

© 1986 David Barrat

Typeset by Hope Services,
Abingdon, Oxfordshire
Printed in Great Britain by
Richard Clay, The Chaucer Press
Bungay, Suffolk

*British Library Cataloguing in
Publication Data*

Barrat, David
Media sociology. – (Society now)
– (Social science paperbacks; 336)
1. Mass media – Social aspects
I. Title II. Series
302.2'34   HM258

ISBN 0 415 05110 X

*Library of Congress Cataloging in
Publication Data*

Barrat, David
Media sociology.
(Society now)
(Social science paperbacks; 336)
Bibliography: p.
Includes index.
1. Mass media – Social aspects.
2. Communication – Social aspects.
I. Title II. Series. III. Series:
Social science paperbacks; 336.
HM258.B375
1986 302.2'34   86-1844

ISBN 0 415 05110 X

Contents

1

Development and approaches

Prologue: seduction of the innocent

YOUTH 'KILLED AFTER A VIDEO SESSION'
(*Daily Mail* headline, 6 July, 1983)

CRUEL MOVIES FAN HACKS 4 TO DEATH
(*Daily Mail* headline, 7 July, 1983)

BAN VIDEO SADISM NOW
(*Daily Mail* headline, 1 July, 1983)

'In some families, apparently, children are actually being
deliberately shown films of buggery, rape and mutilation.
Many see them because they are lying about the home.
This the NSPCC believes is a new form of cruelty. The
organization consulted all its doctors and psychiatrists who
agreed that permanent damage could be done to children's
minds by such pornographic and sadistic material, in
which the detail is powerfully realistic, as in the depiction

of castration or scenes of someone boring through a human skull by an electric drill, bloodily.' (David Holbrook, 'Opinion' article in *Sunday Times*, 2 January, 1983)

From 'nasty' comics to 'video nasties': a case study

The growth in ownership of video tape-recorders has given birth to a new concern about the effects of the media. The so-called 'video nasty', with its graphic depictions of violence and sexuality, has become a major cause for moral campaigners. That these programmes should exert powerful and corrupting effects on children and young people is seen as obvious, as is the need for their legal control.

It is sometimes easier to be objective about contemporary events by seeking historical parallels. Martin Barker's study (1984a) of the campaign against horror comics in Britain in the 1950s provides just such a comparison.

The anti-comic campaign

The comics concerned were originally American imports aimed at adults. They told, in strip cartoon form, stories of crime and horror. They carried titles such as *Tales from the Crypt*, *Crime Detective*, and the more familiar *Superman*. A taste for this style of reading was first acquired as a result of the comics being imported into Britain for US servicemen stationed there.

The campaign against the comics was, in its own terms, a great success. Begun in 1949, it had by 1955 succeeded in getting passed an Act which outlawed their publication. This effectively removed the comics from the shelves of newsagents within weeks.

The history of these events seems simple. A new form of a medium popular among children provokes spontaneous and virtually unanimous protest from all sections of society. Concern is expressed by teachers, magistrates, parents, women's organizations, newspapers, and churches, in public meetings and through professional associations such as the National Union of Teachers (NUT). Pressure groups are established – Barker mentions the Comic Campaign Council and the Council for Children's Welfare – which rapidly mobilize public opinion to the 'obvious need for action':

> The comics were universally condemned. They were badly produced, on poor paper with cheap print. They were full of sadistic violence, horrific obsession with death, lustful representations of women. They showed crime in a glamorous light. Nothing was sacred, everything was corrupt. They could do, must do real damage to their young readers. It was an act of simple morality to stop these fly-by-night publishers.
>
> (Barker 1984a)

The result of pressure from all fronts supported by the recommendation of those professionally concerned with the welfare of children, was the Children and Young Persons (Harmful Publications) Act 1955 whose content was influenced strongly by a draft bill produced by the Comics Campaign Council. The Act was effective despite the fact that the penalties it carried were rarely used. Barker found only one record of a prosecution under the Act and that in 1970 – many years after the 'danger' had passed or been superseded.

The hidden history

Such a straightforward account of the events is, according to Barker, an oversimplification. There is a hidden history, a sub-text to the story. Unknown to many of the participants (and, of course, the general public), there were vested interests behind the campaign. Perhaps the most interesting of these was the role played by the British Communist Party. Ironically – because censorship campaigns are often associated with right-wing politics – the campaign against the comics began within the Communist Party.

Following the war in 1945 the Communist Party set out to win popular support by concentrating their efforts in a campaign against 'American Imperialism'. In Britain the rising tide of 'American world domination' was to be held back by attacking all forms of American influence. Such influence was felt through the economic power of American big business, but also through its effect on British culture, for example in the disciplines of sociology and psychology, in films, music, and, of course, the comics. But the campaign against the comics was just part of this wider political aim.

The effect of the comics on their audience was stated in quite specific terms. The crude and negative stereotypes of foreigners (Germans, Russians, 'Japs', and 'Gooks') that the comics contained, served to justify and legitimate the actions of American soldiers in the real world. It was also claimed that young people raised on such comics would, when older, be psychologically prepared to kill, maim, and torture on behalf of American capitalism. So, according to these critics, the comics performed an important socializing or 'brain-washing' function. Anti-semitic propaganda had served, so it was argued, a similar process in Germany in the 1930s – preparing the way for the emergence of fascism. Later in the campaign such specific theories of the effects of the comics disappeared.

Barker argues that the Communist Party took a very low profile in the subsequent development of the campaign in order to encourage maximum public support for it. As a result most of the openly political arguments were removed from the campaign. The case against the comics became a moral one: the defence of 'national decency'. Very little investigation was carried out into the comics themselves. Their perverse nature and effects were seen to be self-evident. Further research would, therefore, have been unnecessary. Increasingly the appeal was to an outraged common sense of decency:

'Horryfing in extreme. . . . So far fetched, horrifying, disgusting, would be unhealthy for adults . . . joy in crime with a figleaf of morality ... highly improbable and misleading incidents ... misleading mixture of scientific fact and mumbo-jumbo ... Sickly, hypocritical presence of moral at end.'

(Pickard cited in Barker 1984a)

Such observations, published in one of the contemporary 'studies' of the comics, are, of course, moral judgements and not objective or testable findings.

The audience – a neglected group

What of the readers of the comics? Barker argues that they were not mostly children but mainly young adults and predominantly working class. The voice of this readership was never heard during the campaign. Of course such people, on whose behalf changes were being sought, had little access to the channels of influence and publicity that were available to the anti-comics campaigners. In addition their isolation prevented them from putting together any coherent defence. The readers and the reformers came from different social worlds. The reformers were chiefly professional middle-class men and women confronted with a working-class culture which they dismissed as perverted and dangerous. No one sought to discover how the magazines were read and interpreted, or whether the comics actually possessed the qualities of corruption that were attributed to them. Had the reformers attempted to look at the comics as works in their own right they might have come up with a less prejudiced and dismissive appraisal of them. In fact, Barker says that his research convinced him that at least some of them possessed genuine merit, skill, and artistry. But the campaigners did not allow for such a possibility.

Great care was taken to limit the scope of the Act only to the comics. These were defined as publications in which the story is told in pictures, which portray 'crimes or acts of violence or cruelty or incidents of a horrible or repulsive nature' (the Home Secretary introducing the Bill in parliament – quoted in Barker 1984a). Indeed one of the worries raised in the parliamentary debate on the Bill was that the powers that were intended to suppress the comics might be applied elsewhere. But all agreed that the comics themselves were indefensible.

The NUT entered the campaign late, being wary, at first, of what was rightly seen as the political motivation of the campaigners. But as the grounds for objecting to the comics shifted from 'political' to 'common-sense', they put the full force of their professional prestige and influence behind the campaign – with telling results. There were tactical reasons for this last-minute 'conversion'. At a time of pay negotiations the NUT were anxious to establish themselves as *the* professional organization that expressed the interests of children.

Problems of media research

Although not necessarily typical of all media research, what makes the story of the comics campaign in Britain interesting is that it can be used to show many of the dangers, shortcomings, and difficulties which have bedevilled research into the media.

The involvement of outside agencies and pressure groups in much research into the mass media means that researchers must first look carefully at who has sponsored research and what their interests are. This issue is not unique to media research; it occurs in many fields of sociology concerned with 'social problems'.

Moral entrepreneurs

In the case of the horror comics the readers, who were young and working class, lacked the power and organization to challenge the way their consumption of comics was defined as a social problem by the campaigners. It is clear also from

Barker's account that the groups involved in the campaign had their own vested interests. The NUT was trying to maintain its credibility as the professional group concerned with children's welfare, and the British Communist Party sought to use the campaign as a way of broadening its political support among the public. Howard Becker has coined the term 'moral entrepreneur' to describe those who embark on the enterprise of creating and enforcing new rules:

'The prototype of the rule creator ... is the crusading reformer. He is interested in the content of rules. The existing rules do not satisfy him because there is some evil which profoundly disturbs him. He feels that nothing can be right in the world until rules are made to correct it. He operates with an absolute ethic; what he sees is truly and absolutely evil with no qualification. Any means is justified to do away with it. The crusader is fervent and righteous, often self-righteous.'

(Becker 1963: 147–48)

Moral entrepreneurs have played, and continue to play, an important role in pressing for and sponsoring research into mass communication. In Britain the campaign to ban 'video nasties', which has many direct parallels with the anti-comics campaign, provides a recent example of such moral enterprise (see Barker 1984b). As a result much media research has been 'strongly influenced by currents which have little to do with scientific criteria of relevance' (McQuail 1977). There are, of course, other groups and institutions outside the discipline of media studies who have also sponsored a great deal of research. Companies, political parties, and media organizations have all been behind research to discover the effectiveness of their communications. As McQuail concludes:

'Scientific investigations have thus been carried out typically in a context shaped by the practical interests of media producers to achieve their specific aims, or by the concern in society to prevent "harmful" effects. Those "effects" of the media which relate to neither of these have not always been examined with the same zeal. When we come to assess the state of knowledge about the question as a whole we will have to acknowledge a rather large gap on matters which may be most central to understanding the contributions of mass media in modern society.'

(McQuail 1977)

The hypodermic model of the mass media

A second shortcoming found in much of the early research into the mass media can also be illustrated from the example of the comics campaign. This is the belief that the media have almost magical powers to alter the ideas and behaviour of their audience. This is sometimes referred to as the 'hypodermic model' – media messages are seen as being directly injected into the minds of individuals who are powerless to resist. There are two assumptions, common to much of the early research, hidden in this model of the way the media work. The first is often referred to as the idea of 'mass society'. This implies that individuals who make up modern society exist as isolated 'atoms'. This was a view, shared by many early sociologists, that the changes brought about by industrialization had destroyed many of the links between people that were to be found in traditional, pre-industrial communities. This left a society made up of a chaotic mass of individuals who were without any organized community to give their lives shape and meaning. In this world of uncertainty the mass media provided the only point of reference. Mass society produced individuals who were defenceless against the persuasive powers of the media. Media messages pierced the skin with the ease of a hypodermic needle.

Of course, in the case of the comics campaign, the fact that the audience was believed to be made up of children made the persuasive powers of the medium even less resistable. But a concern with the effects of the mass media on children has been a common theme in much other media research too. It appears in more recent work such as Belson (1978) (see pp. 21–6) and the debate in Britain concerning the effect on children of 'video nasties' (see Barker 1984b).

The audience – vulnerable and isolated

The second assumption hidden in the 'hypodermic model' was a rather crude and oversimplified psychological theory of the way in which media messages act on the individual. This too is illustrated by the campaign against comics in Britain.

A book which was important in the British campaign – *Seduction of the Innocent* – was written by an American, Frederic Wertham (1953). He argued that children find the characters in the comics so appealing that they strongly identify with them – coming to see the world through the eyes of the comic characters – with direct effects on behaviour and attitudes:

> 'Superman (with the big S on his uniform – we should be glad, I suppose that it is not an SS) needs an endless stream of ever new submen, criminals, and "foreign looking" people not only to justify his existence, but even to make it possible. It is this feature that engenders in children either one or the other of two possible attitudes: either they fantasy themselves as supermen, with the attendant prejudices against the submen, or it makes them submissive and receptive to the blandishment of strong men who will solve all their social problems for them – by force.'
>
> (Wertham 1953)

Reading Superman forces children into attitudes of dominance or submissiveness. No credit is given to a child's ability to perceive comic characters as unreal or fantasy figures. Whatever is depicted in the comics is accepted as normal and may be copied.

There seems to be a simple equation implied in much of the

research into media effects. Whatever is seen, is then learnt and copied, as Cohen and Young argue:

> 'The dominant model has tended to use a somewhat crude stimulus-response view of human behaviour; the Stimulus (party political broadcast, soapflake commercial, violent drama, sexually explicit film) is measured against a set of direct Responses (voting behaviour, consumer spending, increase of violent crime, sexual offences).'
>
> (Cohen and Young 1981)

If it *were* the case that whatever is depicted in the media is copied, there would be real cause for concern – concern not only about popular culture such as certain films, TV programmes, or videos, but also about 'high' culture. 'Classic' literature and art is not deficient in gruesome deaths and lustful passions, neither are contemporary news, current affairs, and documentary programmes. Yet such products are not usually included in the moral campaigners' proposals for control.

'High' and 'low' culture

One strand of conservative thinking about mass culture has been: 'If it's popular then it must be bad.' In education the argument has gone under the slogan 'more means worse'. The contention here is that to expand education to include the 'masses' will lead to lower standards, an appeal to the 'lowest common denominator', the vulgar and the brash. Such intellectual snobbery is deeply ingrained in much early, and some more recent, media research. But the irony is that once popular tastes have moved on to new forms the middle-class cultural critics have moved in to adopt or 'rediscover' merit in earlier forms of popular culture. Hollywood films, popular music, and jazz have all been made 'respectable' by this process of intellectual upward mobility. But if it's new *and* popular then it's probably worthless and harmful. Even the technology involved in a new medium comes under attack:

'Each campaign against the dangers of a "new" medium always finds reasons to suppose its object is especially dangerous. In the 19th century, Penny Dreadfuls corrupted particularly because they were the only literature their readers could afford. In the early 20th century, films had the big screen, plus the "moral dangers of darkness". Comics could be "pored over" for hours in private. Television is especially bad because it is viewed in the relaxation of one's own home. The videos now carry grave risk because the children can control how they watch. Plus ça change. . .'

(Barker 1983)

Methods: common-sense posing as science

A third shortcoming of much media research that can be illustrated in our account of the comics campaign is the way in which the content of the comics was analysed. The way the campaigners approached the comic was determined to a large extent by their preconceptions. It was self-apparent to them that the comics were indefensible and that they ought to be banned. These were indisputable facts and all that was needed were a few examples to clinch the case. As a result examples were lifted from the comics without any respect for the context in which they occurred.

Most of us would be cautious about condemning all depictions of violence without having regard to the context in which they occur. Certain groups in society such as the police may legitimately use violence in the pursuit of their duties. Is it harmful to depict this? Or is it only the illegitimate use of violence, for example in the depiction of bank robbery, that can have harmful effects? Is it wrong to depict violence that is 'morally justified' – stories of oppressed groups who rise up against their oppressors? Can we all agree on what constitutes an act of violence? Might not some depictions of violence have 'positive effects'? The banned BBC programme 'The War Game' tried, through a vivid account of what might

11

happen if there were a nuclear war in Britain, to persuade people of the dangers of nuclear arms.

Clearly the meanings which we give to violent acts depicted in the media vary according to the context in which they occur and it is reasonable to suppose that this will determine any effect they might have on the audience. Studies which simply tot up the number 'acts of violence' (or swear words, or sexually explicit scenes) are unable to tell us anything useful. In Wertham's work, and that of many other media researchers, the language of science is used to give a gloss of scientific objectivity to what are simply opinions and prejudices as in this account of one of his patients:

> 'Her drawing of a woman showed a masculine type of violent aggressivity. Of average intelligence, she had a reading retardation undoubtedly caused by constant reading of comics.'

> (Quoted in Barker 1984a)

Activity

Read the quotation above carefully and note down some of the sexist assumptions as well as those to do with the alleged effects of comics.

Faulty interpretations

Finally, in their haste to condemn the comics, Barker argues, the campaigners completely misinterpreted the meaning of the strips that they attacked. One much quoted comic strip was described by one of the campaigners as 'an extraordinarily repulsive version of Hansel and Gretel, with one likeable character whom the two children push into an oven and burn to death' (Barker 1983). This was really just an attempt to send up the sentimental nature of fairy stories. Another comic strip frame which achieved much publicity showed an innocent man being chain-whipped to death for being a communist. It was condemned by the paper of the British Communist Party as a piece of anti-communist propaganda typical of the so-called McCarthy era in America. This was in fact a complete misinterpretation of the strip. Barker argues:

'The story as a whole was actually one of a series of brittle and powerful social comment strips (produced by EC Comics). It took the idea that someone could be hypnotized into chain-whipping a communist to death and used it to argue that McCarthyism itself was a piece of mass hypnotism. In other words the real meaning of the story was the exact reverse of what its critics saw in it.'

(Barker 1983)

These are perhaps rather crude examples of media campaigners seeing what they want to see in the comics they wanted to ban. But it does show how difficult it is to interpret any media output. This difficulty has led media research more recently into the area of semiology in an attempt to develop a systematic science of signs and meanings (see pp. 108–17).

Further reading

If you are interested in the anti-comics campaign, Barker's (1984a) book is very readable. Another book edited by the same author (1984b) pursues some of the same arguments in relation to a more contemporary issue: 'video nasties'.

The growth of mass media study

In this last section of the chapter we will look, in outline, at the development of research into mass communication. The *mass media* is a convenient shorthand term usually used to describe all those forms of communication that reach large audiences. It includes film, television, radio, newspapers, magazines, popular literature, and music. Sociological research into the mass media has been uneven. Certain forms have received a good deal of attention, while others have been relatively neglected. In particular, television and the press have been studied much more thoroughly than other forms of mass communication.

The importance of communication

Communication, in all its varied forms, is a topic that is of great interest to sociologists. This is because communication is a precondition of the very existence of a society. Thus it is to be found even in the simple societies of insects such as bees and ants. The honey bee, for example, will communicate the distance and direction of food to other bees in the hive.

Mass communication is a recent development made possible by modern technology. It is a product of industrial techniques such as the steam-powered printing press, cinematography, and radio and TV broadcasting and receiving equipment. For those of us who have access to mass media it is difficult to realize how slowly and inaccurately information was passed around or how little knowledge of the outside world most people possessed before the growth of the mass media. As Marshall McLuhan (1964) has argued, the mass media can be seen as 'extensions of our senses' – they allow us to see and hear beyond our normal sensory limits. But, unlike our predecessors, the bulk of our knowledge is not based on our own direct experience. It is mediated, or received second-hand, via the media. We may know more about drug-takers, film stars, the problems of the Third World, or the national economy, but we have to rely largely on the information on these topics provided by the mass media. As George Gerbner writes:

'Never have so many people in so many places shared so much of a common system of messages and images and have the assumptions about life, society, and the world embedded in them – while having so little to do with their

14

making. The fabric of popular culture that relates elements of existence to each other and structures the common consciousness of what is, what is important, and what is right, is now largely a manufactured product.'

(Gerbner in McQuail 1972)

The media industry

The mass media are products in two senses. They are like other products in that they are the result of an industrial process, and it is interesting to note how much the manufacture of a TV programme or a popular magazine resembles the production of refrigerator or a washing machine. All require the division of labour, a complex social organization, and heavy investment in highly technological capital. And second, we, as consumers, are able to choose only between those products that are available in the market-place. As in other markets the consumer of mass media products has very little control over their nature. One central feature of the mass media is that they are designed to allow a one-way flow of information. A small group of media professionals transmit messages to a much larger audience which has very little opportunity to reply. Writers such as McLuhan take an optimistic view of the mass media, which he sees as possessing the power to reunite mankind in a new electronic community: the 'global village'. Others look more sceptically at the special power of those who control the mass media to manipulate and suppress dissent. Another key feature of the mass media is their speed. They are capable of transmitting the same message simultaneously to a large audience.

Given the importance of the topic, it is surprising that the study of the media has remained, until recently, on the margins of mainstream sociology. Perhaps as a result of this, a variety of different disciplines have contributed to the study of the media. Psychology and especially social psychology have both been concerned. More recently the methods of semiology have been used by students of the mass media. This new science has its origins in yet another discipline – linguistics – the study of language (see pp. 108–17).

Stages of development

It is possible to see three main stages in the development of media study (McQuail 1977: 72–4; Curran and Seaton 1981: 257–89). During the first stage, from the turn of the century until the late 1930s, the media were seen as possessing considerable power to influence behaviour and beliefs. A major contributor to this stage was the Frankfurt school made up of a group of German intellectuals opposed to Hitler. These writers saw the mass media playing a crucial role in the rise of the Nazis. They believed the media were in the process of bringing about a similar transformation in America – where they settled after being forced to leave Germany. Their views resembled what we have called the 'hypodermic' model. In particular they believed that the American mass media were turning individuals into 'masses', destroying culture, and acting as a powerful drug which produced a mindless conformity. The popularity of American mass culture abroad, and particularly in Europe, made this an even greater threat. It is interesting to note that members of the Frankfurt school, which was strongly influenced by Marxist ideas, shared this 'mass manipulative' model of the media with a number of conservative critics of the mass media who believed that high standards could only be kept up if culture was confined to an exclusive élite.

In the second stage of development of media study, from about 1940 to the early 1960s, a much less harmful view of the role of the mass media was emerging from studies in America. Research into the influence of the media on voting behaviour and consumer choice showed that the media appeared to have little or no effect on the attitude and behaviour of the audience. It is important to realize that the idea of 'effect' that was being used here implied an immediate or short-term change. In contrast the writers of the first stage were thinking of much more gradual and long-term influences on behaviour and attitudes. In questioning the power of the mass media, writers in the American tradition stressed the role of social groups – friends, neighbours, and respected opinion leaders – through which media messages were 'filtered'. Thus it was recognized that the audience was not a shapeless 'mass' but belonged to various social groupings. It was necessary to take such intervening variables into account when talking of the effects of the media on individuals. It was also argued that those people who had entrenched views were least likely to be affected by what the media said – only the ignorant and apathetic were likely to be influenced. The position was summed up by Klapper (1960) in the following words: 'mass communication does not ordinarily serve as a necessary and sufficient cause of audience effects, but rather functions through a number of mediating factors.'

But these benign conclusions, though very influential, were based on a smaller number of studies in a narrow range of areas. Much of the work of researchers within this tradition was based on experimental studies and surveys whose methodology is now suspect. As we shall see later, critics have questioned whether such conclusions can be generalized to all aspects of media influence.

Finally, looking at the third stage in the development of research into the mass media, there appear to be several connected trends. First, the search for effects, though not abandoned, has been put into a less prominent place – partly because so much research in stage two came to the conclusion that the media had little or no effect. As one review has it: 'All that is left is a research tradition which has proved relatively barren within its own terms and which has stunted theoretical development within the field' (Curran, Gurevitch, and Woollacott 1977: 3). More recently the focus of research has shifted to the *content* of the mass media. Cohen and Young's (1981) influential collection of articles on the media argued that effects were a secondary issue. Concentrating on the way in which the media select and present information, they relegated 'effects' to a final and brief section at the end of their book. This was not because the search for effects could be dismissed an unimportant. But, they argued, few studies did justice to the complex ways in which the mass media affect their audiences.

Media researchers have developed a more sophisticated set of techniques to analyse the content of the media and these will be discussed more fully in Chapter 4. A second major theme of recent research has been the *process* of media production. This had led to studies of media organizations, their day-to-day operation, and the wider social, economic, and political structure within which they work. This is dealt with more fully in Chapter 3. Finally the study of effects has broadened out to include effects on knowledge as well as on attitudes, long-term as well as short-term effects, and the power of the media to determine the framework within which issues are discussed and decided. Chapter 2 takes up the issue of effects over a number of key areas of enquiry.

Further reading

There are few easy accounts of the development of mass media research, and many of the textbooks meant for the beginner in sociology ignore the topic altogether. If you wish to read further, the introductions to the three main sections of Cohen and Young's (1981) book are a good starting-point, or you could try the article by McQuail (1977). You will have to work at both of these.

John Fiske's book (Fiske 1982) is also a useful introduction to this rapidly growing discipline.

2
Effects

In the 'chequered' history of media research since its origins at the turn of the century, the idea of the 'effects' of the media has played an important part. But at each stage in the development of media study, researchers saw 'effects' in quite different ways. In the first stage effects were perceived on a grand scale as dramatic and far-reaching, but their impact was assumed; little work went into trying to measure them.

The second stage of media study – developed by American sociologists in the 1940s and 1950s – came to quite opposite conclusions. Through a series of empirical studies they claimed to show that the media had very limited direct effects. The power of the media was moderated by the intervening influence of social groups. Media effects were indirect.

In the last twenty years research into the 'effects' of the media has taken a less prominent position. The reason for this is not, as the American sociologists of the 1940s and 1950s believed, that the media have little effect, but that media effects have to be more broadly defined and researched using more sophisticated analytical tools. The task is to uncover the subtle ways in which the media work – through, for example, images of deviance, stereotypes, and agenda-setting.

'Sex and violence'

The 'hypodermic' model of media effects is not dead. Although it has been decisively criticized by many media researchers, it still lives on as a common-sense theory (often popularized by the press themselves) and underpins the activity of moral campaigners who seek to censor the output of the mass media for the 'benefit' of their audiences. Nowhere is this model more alive than in the controversy over the effects on audiences – particularly young audiences – of scenes of violence and sexuality. Although it is now of marginal interest to most media researchers it is the area of research that continues to attract most publicity, official inquiries, and commissions – and large research funds for those social scientists who are prepared to do further research in the area. Media sociologists have not abandoned a concern with the effects of the media. In recent years, for example, feminism has highlighted the effects on male behaviour of media depictions of sexuality and violence and their consequences for women. Most media sociologists are now, however, sceptical of the over-simple explanations of the hypodermic model.

The media and delinquency

By far the most common form of research into the effects of 'sex and violence' in the media has been to seek to show how it is a cause of juvenile delinquency. This alleged link between popular culture and delinquency has a long history. As the case of the horror comics illustrates, a number of different forms of popular culture have been accused of being a contributory cause of juvenile delinquency. Graham Murdock and Robin McCron (1979), in an assessment of recent

20

research in this area, found that very similar accusations were being made in an article they quote from – published in 1851!

> 'One powerful agent for the depraving of the boyish classes of our towns and cities is to be found in the cheap shows and theatres, which are so specially chosen and arranged for the attraction and ensnaring of the young. When for three-pence a boy can procure some hours of vivid enjoyment from exciting scenery, music and acting . . . it is not to be wondered at that the boy who is led on to haunt them becomes rapidly corrupted and demoralized, and seeks to be the doer of the infamies which have interested him as a spectator.'
>
> (*Edinburgh Review*, quoted in Murdock and McCron 1979)

Although here it is not TV but cheap theatres in working-class areas that were held to be the cause of juvenile delinquency, more recently Hollywood films and pop music have also been blamed for youthful crime.

Research in this area has largely cut itself off from other sociological studies of juvenile delinquency. Rather than look at the role of factors such as class, subculture, and the activity of the police, they concentrate doggedly on the single issue of exposure to media sexuality and violence. The popularity of this sort of explanation, in which the media are made the scapegoat of all society's ills, may well be that it stops us going further to ask awkward questions about, for example, inequalities of wealth and opportunity.

We have chosen two representative examples of this approach to discuss: Eysenck and Nias's (1980) recent survey of the psychological literature and William Belson's (1978) detailed survey based on interviews with London boys. These represent the two major methods employed in gathering evidence to justify the claim that media sex and violence affect behaviour. The experimental method is favoured by Eysenck and Nias – 'From the point of view of testing scientific theories in a rigorous manner . . . experimental laboratory

21

studies are, without doubt, the method of choice' (Eysenck and Nias 1980) – whereas Belson opts for a field study. Because field studies are conducted in a natural environment rather than the controlled environment of the laboratory they are able to take account of sociological factors. The experiment, on the other hand, is more concerned with the psychology of the individual. But both Eysenck and Nias and Belson come to similar conclusions – that the media can have harmful effects and may contribute to crime and delinquency or sexual 'perversion'. And for both parties this constitutes 'scientific' support for further censorship of depictions of acts of violence and sexuality.

The experimental approach

Eysenck and Nias's review emphasizes the psychological evidence and largely ignores sociological facts. Their ideal form of research is the controlled laboratory experiment. Only here, they feel, is it possible to be in sufficient control of the situation to be able to produce quantitative and therefore 'scientific' results. Murdock and McCron summarize this technique thus:

'Laboratory experiments have been very widely used in research on television and violence and most follow the same basic design. You take a group of people and divide them into two (sometimes three) sub-groups, either by assigning them at random so that everyone has an equal chance of ending up in either group, or by trying to match them so that both groups have the same basic composition. You might, for example, want to ensure that both groups had an equal number of men and women, middle and working class subjects, introverts and extroverts, or whatever factors you felt were relevant. Both groups are then shown a piece of film. The so-called "experimental" group is shown a sequence featuring violence (almost always inter-personal) while the "control" group watch a

22

"neutral" piece, or co-operative behaviour. The responses of both groups are then measured. A variety of techniques have been tried from charting physiological changes during viewing (blood pressure, sweating and so on) to observing social behaviour directly afterwards to see if subjects behave more aggressively.'

(Murdock and McCron 1979)

Experiments such as these show fairly consistent evidence of direct and powerful effects. Eysenck and Nias liken the media researcher's use of laboratory experiments to the aircraft designer's use of a wind tunnel or heat chamber to test aeroplane prototypes. Only when the basic design problems of media 'sex and violence' research have been ironed out in the laboratory will the research designer be able to 'test fly' research in the field.

Limitations of the experiment

It is true that engineers can predict quite accurately the performance of a full-size aircraft from the behaviour of a model in a design laboratory – but human beings are not so uniform or inanimate. Their behaviour, unlike the aircraft's performance, depends on a whole web of relationships and meanings that result from day-to-day experience within a particular culture. Sociologists (and increasingly many psychologists too) see little value in the use of laboratory experiments which tear human behaviour from its social context. Can we be sure that the results are not due to the subjects doing what they believe the experimenter wants? There is a large body of evidence that such effects can often spoil results. Do we have enough information to 'control' for all relevant factors that might contribute to the final outcome? Most importantly, how much do these results – obtained under 'hygienic' laboratory conditions – tell us about what people may do in a real but 'dirty' world? They have an appealing simplicity and elegance and they offer the lure of

23

'scientific respectability', but this is achieved at the cost of a very narrow vision of human behaviour.

Criticizing research of this sort is not the same as saying that the mass media cannot be the cause of violent behaviour. But such effects are rarely as direct and immediate as a mechanical 'response' to a media 'stimulus'. Further, as we have already argued in relation to the horror comics, it is not possible to define 'violence' (still less 'sexual perversion') in the abstract – outside the context in which it occurs in a media product. One can only wonder how the subjects of such experiments struggled to interpret the brief film clips, slides, etc. of 'violent' or 'sexual' behaviour – usually without the context of a plot to 'make sense' of such acts. What is clear is that the experimentalists are not in the least concerned with how subjects interpret stimulus materials. For them, the interpretation of such materials is obvious.

Finally, the mechanism of effect that is implied in these experiments is a simple 'you see it and then you do it' reflex. It is based on a mindless image of human action. Certainly mass media products may trigger off behaviour in 'disturbed' individuals who are already predisposed to such actions:

'A fifteen year old girl attempted to murder her parents by cutting the brakes of the family car after getting the idea from "Starsky and Hutch". The attempt went wrong when she came out of school and was horrified to find her parents waiting to drive her home! In the week before the murder attempt, the girl was reported to have become immersed in crime fiction, reading novels by Agatha Christie and Alfred Hitchcock.'

(Eysenck and Nias 1980: 67)

Case studies such as this, based on clinical reports, are often used by moral entrepreneurs such as Mary Whitehouse as evidence of the need for censorship. However, as the example above neatly illustrates, the girl was already on a course of action – what 'Starsky and Hutch' could not provide Agatha Christie might. There is little justification for, or sense in, trying to 'clean up' all popular culture for such a minority of individuals. As Eysenck and Nias themselves conclude, such case study evidence 'is scientifically of least interest, and probably largely lacking in the power of proof' (1980:65). It is worth observing that some psychological studies have come to the opposite conclusion, that far from causing 'unacceptable' social behaviour, the mass media offer a harmless outlet or 'safety valve' for 'anti-social' behaviour – though Eysenck and Nias reject the evidence on which these inconvenient findings are based.

Within the simple experimental model of media cause and effect it is not possible to see how the mass media might cause violence by misinformation – perhaps by inciting racial hatred or contempt for women. Or, as Murdock and McCron (1979) argue, the media may emphasize inequalities. The differences between the exotic lifestyles depicted in 'Dallas' or popular romantic fiction and the drab reality of daily life experienced by many who make up the audience for such products may cause frustration and aggression. Such 'effects', which may be very 'real', are beyond the reach of the experimental approach.

Not all of those who adopt a psychological approach to the study of the media take such a negative view of their effects. Television can be used to encourage reading and literacy as well as to teach the newer skills of 'visual literacy' (see Greenfield (1984) for a recent survey of research in this vein).

The field study

William Belson's study seems more likely to receive serious attention from sociologists. He has a long experience of media research including working in the BBC Audience Research Department and conducting research, for the London Press Exchange, into the effects of television on the reading and buying of newspapers and magazines. He has also done research on juvenile delinquency and so is familiar with the sociological arguments in this area (Belson 1967, 1975).

Belson's approach is a quantitative field study based on interviews with 1,565 boys aged between 12 and 17 conducted in the early 1970s. His study seeks to establish a link between the boys' television viewing habits and their involvement in violence and juvenile crime.

The boys' tastes in television were measured by checking their recall of a sample of 100 programmes broadcast between 1959 and 1971. One difficulty with this procedure was that it required the boys to remember programmes which were broadcast when some of the younger ones were still babies. The programmes were scored on a ten-point scale for their violence. This scoring was done by a group of middle-class adults. Accordingly the sample excluded programmes that the adults could not recall – although among these may have been programmes that had a great effect on the boys.

Violence

Adopting a broad definition of 'violence'. Belson asked the boys to report any violent behaviour that they had been involved in during the previous six months. How should such self-reports of violence be evaluated? A detailed questionnaire was put to a cross-section of people – with rather mixed results. One item asked how violent is 'scratching the paint on a new car with a knife'? For 18 per cent this was 'very' or 'extremely' violent, but another 21 per cent felt that it was only 'a bit' or 'slightly' violent. It seems that among the general public there is a good deal of room for disagreement about what is a violent act. One reason for this variability may be that our assessment of violence in the real world (as in the media) depends on the situation in which it occurs.

Taking this into account would have made accurate measurement very complicated if not impossible, so Belson insisted that the boys' acts of violence be assessed independently of the situation in which they occurred – thereby risking quite serious errors. He ends up with a measure of 'serious' violence which ranges from 'I busted the telephone in a telephone box'

26

to 'I deliberately hit a boy in the face with a broken bottle' or 'I fired a revolver at someone'.

Using data collected on the boys, their television viewing, and their involvement in violent behaviour, Belson arrives at the conclusion that 'high exposure to television violence increases the degree to which boys engage in serious violence'. Murdock and McCron argue that this conclusion could only have been reached by taking a very narrow view of the problem and ignoring a number of relevant factors. Indeed, they point out that Belson's own data show that while both middle and working-class boys watched violent programmes their levels of violent behaviour were quite different:

'Thirty nine per cent of the boys from middle class homes fell in the high exposure group as against 41% of those from lower working class families. But his result showed also that involvement in "serious" violence did vary significantly with class background. Whereas only 13% of boys from higher non-manual families admitted committing four or more "serious" acts, the figure for those from lower working class homes was almost three times as high, 38%.'
(Murdock and McCron 1979)

Also, the keenest viewers of television violence were *not* the highest scorers in violent behaviour (perhaps this could be taken to mean that a forced diet of violent television would *reduce* juvenile delinquency!)

Belson does not use his data to assess the effect of television in relation to other already established causes of delinquency: social class, the school, the local community, etc. Referring to other research, Murdock and McCron conclude that violent behaviour can only be understood in the context of a 'male street culture rooted in the working class neighbourhood' and that the mass media have an effect only via this subculture.

Other studies

Not all studies of the effects of violence in the media make use of the 'hypodermic' model. George Gerbner has recently conducted research to show that characters in television drama encounter more personal violence than the typical viewer. This affects the way viewers perceive reality. Viewers were asked to say which of two different statements about social violence is correct. One set reflected official statistics of crime, the other the levels of crime shown on television. Heavy viewers of television were more likely to choose the over-estimated 'television' statistics than light viewers. These beliefs were reflected too in behaviour. Heavy viewers were more mistrustful of others and more likely to fear walking alone in the city streets at night. The television picture of the world provides these viewers with a definition of reality which is more powerful than personal experience (Gerbner *et al.* 1979).

A number of studies carried out by mainly Marxist researchers in Britain during the 1970s into the effects of media portrayals of violence have taken the line that they serve to legitimize the forces of law and order, to scapegoat outsiders, and thus to draw together the rest of society (e.g. Cohen 1972; Hall *et al.* 1978; Chibnall 1977). These studies are dealt with more fully later (see pp. 36–57).

'The Audience Strikes Back'

> 'We must get away from the habit of thinking in terms of what the media do to people and substitute for it the idea of what the people do with the media.'
>
> (Halloran 1970)

As we have said, in the 1940s and 1950s a major shift took place in the way the effects of the mass media were perceived. A new and influential approach to studying the mass media emerged which looked much more closely at the role of the audience. A major purpose of this new approach, which became the second phase in the development of media study, was to deny the mass media the sort of all-embracing impact which earlier writers ascribed to them. Individuals were no longer seen as a 'mass of isolated atoms' who were unable to resist the persuasion of the media.

Selective perception

This American school of thought came to the conclusion that the audience could look after themselves. They stressed the defences, both social and psychological, that protected the audience from the mass media. On a psychological level, it was argued, individuals were not simply 'taken in' by the media. Members of the audience would instead respond to the message selectively. Where an opinion was expressed which fitted in with their personal beliefs this would be accepted, but equally, ideas that contradicted strongly held beliefs would be rejected. So the idea of an audience that was made of helpless individuals was decisively contested. This recognition that what the media said could mean different things to different people was an advance on the passive view of the audience subscribed to in the earlier accounts of mass media effects. It has subsequently been developed into a model of media effects known as the 'uses and gratifications' theory. This argues that different people satisfy different needs from the mass media; that different social groups may give quite different interpretations of the same media product, be it a radio soap opera, a television quiz programme, or a news story.

Groups filter messages

As members of social groups the audience possessed a second 'line of defence' against the powers of mass media persuasion. Empirical studies of consumer and political choice seemed to indicate that the influence of the mass media was only indirect. Individuals were more affected by the people and groups around them – friends, neighbours, workmates – than by the output of the mass media. On each issue each social group has a small number of key individuals who were regarded as an 'authority' – whether it was a question of fashion or politics. Such respected 'opinion leaders' were sought out by individual group members – and their opinions were highly influential. The opportunities for the media to influence the mass audience were seen to be very limited because the process was so indirect – ideas 'flow from the radio and print to the opinion leaders and from them to the less active sections of the population' (Katz and Lazarsfeld 1956). This model of the effects of the media became known as the 'two-step flow of communications'.

Between the first and second stage in the development of media study the pendulum swung from the view that the media had massive effects on its audience to the opposite view that the media had very limited effects. The 'limited effects' conclusion is one to which few media researchers would now subscribe, although it is still popular among media professionals who use it to argue that they 'just give the public what it wants'. For this reason Stan Cohen and Jock Young (1981) have labelled this the 'market' or 'commercial' model. Critics have questioned the findings, the theoretical assumptions, and the research methods of the approach. However, it did show the need for empirical work and the importance of understanding what the audience *does* with a media product.

'Two-step flow'

The 'two-step flow' model was first put forward in a study by Lazarsfeld, Berelson, and Gaudet (1944) of the 1940 American presidential election. It concluded that the decisions of electors were little influenced by political views expressed in the mass media. The study emphasized the 'loyalty' of most electors to their chosen party. Party allegiances were, it was claimed, established early in life and remained stable. Only a minority of the electors, about a quarter, made their minds up during the presidential campaign and, if anything, these 'floating voters' paid less attention to the political messages

30

broadcast in the mass media than the 'stable' voters. Instead the major 'effect' of the political messages of the mass media was to reinforce what voters already knew and believed. Voters *used* the mass media selectively. Political propaganda simply rallied the faithful – it did not produce converts. Trenaman and McQuail's (1961) later study of the British general election campaign of 1959 came to very similar conclusions. The swing to the Conservative Party was 'neither related to the degree of exposure nor to any particular programmes or arguments put forward by the parties' (Trenaman and McQuail 1961: 191).

The two-step flow model was given its fullest expression in a second study by Lazarsfeld (Katz and Lazarsfeld 1956). This was an assessment of the influence of the media in four 'issue areas': the political decisions of voters, and the choice of consumer products, films, and fashions. The groups studied were all women and the importance of opinion leaders was confirmed. Personal influence far outweighed the media in determining the choices individuals made whether it was which breakfast cereal to buy, what film to see, or who to vote for in an election. The American ideal of democracy seemed safe. Not only were the media *not* very influential, it was found too that opinion leaders were *not* necessarily the wealthy and the powerful high-status members of society. Different people were the leaders of opinion in different areas of choice – power was in no way concentrated in the hands of any particular group or élite. The pluralist idea of power dispersed across the population was apparently verified.

Criticisms

Since the 1960s many criticisms have been directed against this research. The conclusion of limited effects was hasty and overgeneralized. It is reasonable to assume that the choice of a fashion, a film, a consumer product, or a presidential candidate each follows the same sort of process? Even if they do, can it be concluded from the limited effect of the media in these areas that the media have only limited effects on all *other* aspects of our lives? Katz and Lazarsfeld's own findings showed, for example, that the women in their sample found it harder to say which people influenced them on political matters than on the other three areas. They also found that 58 per cent of the changes in political choice that occurred among voters could *not* be attributed to personal influence 'and were often very dependent on the mass media'. But this contradictory evidence of substantial media effects in the case of political choice was ignored in their general conclusions.

The 'effects' of the media were defined in a narrow short-term way in order to make it easy to measure them. It is not surprising that a limited *definition* of effects gives rise to a finding of 'limited effects'. For example, by defining political effects in terms of changes in support during an election campaign they ruled out the possibility of longer-term influences being at work. But evidence exists of short-term media influences in the area of politics. In 1968, the British MP Enoch Powell gave a speech to a small audience in a church hall concerning the 'dangers' of immigration. Two days later, as a result of extensive media coverage, 86 per cent of the population knew about the speech:

'Before the speech only 6% of a Gallup poll sample thought immigration was an issue of national importance. Afterwards 27% thought it was important, and nearly 70% of the public believed that the government would have to take a "harder line".'

(Curran and Seaton 1981: 273)

The issue of immigration was rapidly turned into a prominent feature of political debate in the short term. The mass media also set the agenda for the type of discussion about race that was to take place in succeeding years. A major feature of this was the 'numbers game'. Debate centred around claims and counter-claims to the statement that there were 'too many foreign [meaning black] immigrants in Britain' and that 'they' threatened to 'overrun' both the physical and cultural environment. This sort of political role of the media was outside the definition of political effect used by Lazarsfeld and his followers.

The mass media may also have political effects through its 'non-political' output. For example, the 'information' provided by racial stereotypes in popular fiction, television drama, or advertisement may have an effect on the political attitude of the audience towards such groups.

The methods of social psychology had a strong influence on these early studies. Techniques of measurement, statistical methods of survey sampling and data analysis, developed by social psychologists, were taken as the model for scientific enquiry by Lazarsfeld. A psychological definition of power was also employed. Power was defined as a direct process of influence – the power of one individual over another. Such a definition of power makes it impossible to see power as part of the social structure related to social class, institutions, and economic processes. Neither is it possible to see power as control over ideas – ideological power.

The conclusion that the mass media simply reinforced what people already believed was taken by Lazarsfeld and his colleagues to support the idea that the media had limited effects. But in reinforcing existing opinions the media may be preventing change taking place and preserving the existing structure of society. Keeping things the same is just as much a real effect as causing change to occur. This is especially relevant if the status quo benefits some sections of society at the expense of others. Of course, Lazarsfeld, along with many of his contemporary sociologists, held to the functionalist view that society *was* an orderly and unchanging whole that worked for the mutual benefit of everyone. But increasingly sociologists who are sceptical of the assumptions of functionalism have begun to ask: whose interests are being served by the mass media's support for the status quo?

The rediscovery of effects

Sociologists are now less willing to conclude that the mass media have few political effects. One reason is that party loyalty is clearly weaker than it was in the 1940s and 1950s. Fewer voters are willing to vote for the same political party throughout their lives. Linked to this change is a weakening of the connection between social class position and patterns of party allegiance.

Second, since the time of the 'limited effects' studies, the technology of mass communications has changed significantly. Television has become, for many of the audience, the most important source of news and information – especially during election periods. In America where, unlike Britain, few restrictions exist on electoral spending on political advertising, election campaigns are conducted primarily through the media. Blumler (1979) has shown that television is the main source of electoral information for over 70 per cent of the electorate. The growing popularity of television as a medium has exposed even those least interested in political messages: 'Large numbers of people are watching election broadcasts not because they are interested in politics but because they like watching television' (Katz 1971).

More recently attention has shifted to the ideological significance of all media products, not only those carrying an overt political message. This was paralleled by a shift in other research away from the earlier notion of *persuasion* (with its implications of direct effects, and intentional political communications) to a view of the media as a supplier of *information*.

Recent theories of media effects have not returned to the earlier view of an audience composed of easily manipulated puppets. A number of British studies have shown how the response of audiences to the mass media is guided by the groups and subcultures to which they belong (McRobbie and Garber 1976; Cohen and Robins 1978; Willis 1978). Dorothy Hobson (1980) shows how the use housewives make of the radio reflects their social situation. One such feature of the housewife's experience is a relative lack of structure. Unlike many employed workers, the housewife has a fair degree of choice about how and when housework is done. Many of Hobson's sample of working-class housewives had the radio on all day while they were doing housework and the radio programmes helped to structure their day. The programming of popular radio shows an awareness of this function, with breakfast and lunchtime shows, and mid-morning and mid-afternoon breaks where listeners may be recommended to 'put their feet up'.

Activity

Read through the following transcripts of interviews conducted with two women (Pat and Anne) by Dorothy Hobson (D):

'Pat: I like Radio 1. Tony Blackburn. I think he's corny but I think he's good. Dave Lee Travis I like and Noel Edmonds. Noel Edmonds, I think he's absolutely fantastic. . . .

D: So do you prefer the radio?

P: During the day, yes.

D: Would you have the radio on while you were doing housework?

P: Oh yes, yes.

D: Why do you like the people you like?

P: Er . . . their personality – it comes over on the radio. Noel Edmonds, I think he's really fantastic, you know . . . I think he's really lovely (laughs).

D: And do you do your housework at the same time?

P: Oh yes.

Anne: I listen to BRMB [a local radio station], you know, that's quite a good programme. I like listening to the people that phone in, er . . . I like the conversations.

D: Why do you think that is?

A: Er . . . I suppose its because I'm on me own.

D: Is it the music as well that you like or . . .?

A: Yes, 'cos I find that nearly all my records are a bit old-fashioned and I like to hear a bit of the modern music . . . I don't want to get behind the times, you know.'

(Hobson 1980)

1 Make a list of the different uses of radio that are suggested by the answers given by Pat and Anne.

2 How are these uses connected to the experience of these women as young, newly married, working-class housewives?

3 Try interviewing members of another social group with which you are familiar to see whether listening (or viewing or reading habits) can be linked to their social situation.

Reporting rumours, amplifying 'deviance'

Looking at the mass media as 'amplifiers of deviance' is a relatively recent approach – a spin-off from recent sociological ideas about crime and 'deviance'. When sociologists use the term 'deviance amplification' they are not just referring to the obvious point that the mass media frequently exaggerate what happens in the real world. They are describing a media 'effect' – a process by which fictional and non-fictional representations of 'deviance' are able to 'feedback' on to the perceptions and behaviour of individuals. The outcome of this process is often an apparent increase in the amount of 'deviance'.

But the connection between deviance and the mass media is not just an academic one. The media have always had a taste for the bizarre, the exotic, and the outrageous, whether in the form of fiction or 'hard news'.

Activity

You can prove for yourself the importance of 'deviant' behaviour for the media by a simple content analysis. Take an edition of a popular daily newspaper and classify the content into two categories: items concerned with 'deviance', and other items. (You can do this by simply measuring with a ruler the amount of space devoted each item.) You can, of course, extend this exercise by looking at other newspapers and other media (TV, radio, etc.). You may find it useful to refer to the section of content analysis in Chapter 4 (p. 103).

The occurrence of 'moral panics' concerning particular forms of 'deviance' is a topic that has been mainly studied with reference to news reports of deviance. Fictional forms of deviance (presented in films, television, and popular novels) have unfortunately received less attention from media sociologists, although there is a strong case for expecting that images of deviance conveyed by this sort of media product also have significant effects. Jerry Palmer (1973) argues that the characterization of the villain in popular thrillers serves to legitimate in the public eye the use by the police of 'dirty tricks'. In a world populated by committed and ruthless criminals, the police cannot afford to be hamstrung by bureaucratic, legal niceties if they are to preserve 'our' safety. The violent detective hero, exemplified by the Clint Eastwood 'Dirty Harry' character, is justified in his 'shoot first and ask questions later' style. It is through such tales, Palmer argues, that we are invited to accept the view that the police cannot be expected to observe legal safeguards and civil liberties – or even the law itself – if they are to rid the world of villainy.

Of course it is not only in modern industrial society that rumours spread through the social fabric, neither is there anything new in such rumours depicting certain groups in a negative and distorted fashion. Rumours, which titillate the imagination and defame the innocent, arise in any social organization. But the rumours involved in the deviancy amplification process are much more authoritative and entail much more serious consequences.

As Cohen and Young (1981: 429) have argued, the 'moral

37

panic', unlike a rumour, is not a process everyone can join in 'democratically', contributing their own slant on the message like a game of Chinese whispers. This is partly the result of what we described earlier (see p. 15) as a defining feature of mass communication: it is a *one-way* process of communication. And there is no guarantee of equal access; the views of the powerful occupy a privileged position in the media. In the case of reports of 'deviance' it is the official view that is most likely to get aired in the media: the opinions of judges and magistrates, of members of parliament and senators, of police chiefs and senior officers, and of those public figures who claim a mandate as the 'moral guardians' of society. By contrast we are rarely given the first-hand accounts of 'deviants' themselves. Their experiences, problems, behaviours, and motivations are explained to us by others on their behalf. In short, there is what Becker has described as a 'hierarchy of access' to the media, and those whose behaviour is most frequently reported (the poor, the powerless, and the 'deviant') have the least rights over what is said.

'In any system of ranked groups, participants take it as given that members of the highest group have the right to define the way things really are . . . those at the top have access to a more complete picture of what is going on than anybody else. Members of lower groups will have incomplete information and their view of reality will be partial and distorted in consequence.'

(Becker 1967)

The authority of the mass media in reporting rumours about deviants is strengthened by the fact that, in a complex society, we cannot check media allegations against experience. Most of us live out our lives within a small segment of the larger society. The range of people we meet and events we experience directly is relatively small (see p. 14). Leslie Wilkins, author of the term 'deviancy amplification', argues that most of us do not have direct contact with those who are labelled in society as 'deviant'. We may feel we know all

38

about the 'mugger', the 'dope-fiend', or the 'juvenile delinquent', and we may indeed have access to a large stock of 'knowledge' about such groups and activities. But this knowledge differs in quality from the direct experience of deviance in pre-industrial communities:

> 'In earlier times the young and the old were continuously in touch with each other; youth was aware of the problems of age, and age was aware of the problems of youth. The village was aware of the problems of mental deficiency — each village had its village idiot who was part of the total culture.'

> (Wilkins 1981:37)

But the 'village idiot' of today is kept in special institutions. Our knowledge of insanity and the insane is second-hand and not direct, although we may know more about the 'types' and 'causes' of insanity than our forebears. The greater knowledge we may now have of deviance is one-dimensional. It derives from the one-sided accounts given to us by the media which, because they are based on official views, see 'deviance' as 'obviously' wrong and equally obviously something to be controlled or eradicated.

More recently sociologists have taken the view that deviance may, in part, be caused by the reaction that society has towards certain types of behaviour. The notion of 'deviance amplification' highlights the role played by the media in this.

Sensitization

As a result of their relative social isolation, the police rely to a large extent on the mass media as a barometer of public opinion. If particular forms of crime and deviance are presented there as matters of great concern (urban crime and 'mugging', drug-taking, or street demonstrations, for example) then the police will respond by focusing their attention on such people and activities. They become particularly sensitive to signs of such behaviour from among all those they could attend to. And because within any community there exists a large amount of undetected crime, such focusing produces more arrests.

The courts also become sensitized to issues raised in the media and respond with sentences of increased severity. The public too are put on the alert for particular forms of deviance. Part of the process of sensitization is the way in which certain styles of dress and objects are elevated into visible symbols of deviance. Thus skin colour, hairstyles, motor bikes, and leather jackets have all been used as a kind of symbolic shorthand for recognizing 'troublemakers'. During a moral panic, news reports may carry stylized images that emphasize these symbols of deviance. And of course the deviants themselves, and many others who 'appear' to fall into the same category, are spun out of the world of 'respectable' society into the deep space of the 'outsider' by the accelerating spiral or moral panic.

At each stage the mass media are involved in fanning the flames of public concern. The focusing of police activity and its consequences (higher rates of detected crime) become newsworthy in themselves – '50% MORE MUGGINGS', 'POLICE CRACK DOWN ON HEROIN'. So too do the responses of the courts – 20 WAR PROTESTORS JAILED', 'WE MUST STAMP OUT THIS EVIL SAYS JUDGE'. And, in this second circuit of the spiral, such reports serve only to confirm and reinforce both the police and the courts in their 'tougher' response. As the moral panic spirals on, official rates of crime and deviance rise, increasing numbers of people become marginalized in 'deviant' roles, the police adopt harsher methods, and the courts impose stiffer penalties.

Moral panics concerning a number of types of 'deviant' behaviour and persons have been studied in some detail – 'mugging' (Hall *et al.* 1978), anti-war demonstrators (Halloran *et al.* 1968), welfare claimants (Golding and Middleton 1982), drug-taking (Young 1971), mid-sixties youth groupings –

'Mods and Rockers' (Cohen 1972), and football 'hooliganism' (Marsh, Rosser, and Harré 1978).

Societal reaction

Common to each of the above studies is the view that the 'societal reaction', replayed via the mass media, exaggerates and distorts reality. Welfare claimants are depicted as cunning and idle rogues whose fraudulent schemes exploit the honest and hard-working taxpayer; marijuana users are seen as indistinguishable from heroin addicts; and political demonstrations are shown to be manipulated by groups of revolutionary militants intent on violence.

A gallery of such folk devils is assembled for our inspection and edification, and although individual exhibits may change the show goes on. All the groups stigmatized in this way are relatively powerless – the young, the poor, and the outsiders.

Common to all these studies also is the view that these folk devils are just the visible symptom of deeper and less obvious disagreements and conflicts in society.

What turns the amplifier on?

How do such amplification cycles begin and end? Answers to this are to be found partly in the wider social and political context – the ideological climate in which the process occurs – and partly within the operation of the media themselves. The 'news sense' of editors and reporters lead them to believe that public interest in particular folk devils can only be sustained for a limited period. New angles on a jaded story are sought out but eventually it is dropped for fear of becoming repetitive. And in some cases the behaviour simply 'goes away' – the media could not hope to keep alive the 'Mods and Rockers' mythology when the young people themselves had abandoned these forms of youthful rebellion for others: 'hippies', 'skinheads', 'punks', etc. Nevertheless many other stories appear to have an enduring fascination for the media –

41

'muggers', 'football hooligans', and 'welfare scroungers' recur as regular themes over longer periods. Such persistence requires ideological perspectives which are being investigated by research into stereotypes and agenda-setting.

Activity

Moral panics do not only occur on a national scale but also within local communities. Local media, both newspapers and radio, often run campaigns on issues which may range from 'juggernauts' to 'gypsies'. These provide an ideal opportunity for small-scale research. In particular look out for:

1 Distortion and exaggeration, inaccuracies in reporting and language ('military' and 'animal' analogies are common).
2 The classification of unconnected events under the umbrella of the 'deviant' label.
3 Evidence of 'official' responses (societal reaction) and policy changes.
4 The relative space given to different groups (hierarchy of access).
5 Evidence of 'effects' on the behaviour and self-concepts of those who are labelled.

Stereotypes

The concept of stereotype, as a kind of 'blinkered' mental attitude, is a notion imported into media study from psychology. As a result the concept has involved a number of assumptions more relevant to psychology, whose main focus is on the individual. These assumptions have caused difficulties for sociologists concerned with the effects of stereotypes on media audiences. In particular, some reworking of the concept has been necessary to enable analysis of the ideological role of stereotypes.

The stereotype notion is clearly linked in some ways to the sociological notion of deviant labels (see previous section, pp. 36–42). But the concept of the label is more clearly defined. We know more about the processes that produce labels and about their origins in the structures of power and authority in society.

Deviant labels are descriptions or versions of behaviour that undermine and devalue that behaviour – they dismiss it as irrational ('mindless militants', 'senseless vandalism'). They are usually negative and, as the new sociologists of deviance were at pains to point out, their consequence was often to increase deviance and strengthen deviant identities.

By contrast stereotypes frequently attempt to validate certain roles and behaviour. Far from being necessarily negative (though some are) they often present us with positive models of behaviour to emulate. The 'housewife' stereotype, common in TV programmes, films, magazines, news stories, and especially favoured by advertisers, is a role women are invited to copy and men to reinforce. But both stereotypes and labels reflect power relations in the wider society and both exist as powerful forces in the real world as well as being reinforced through the media.

The psychological view of the stereotype

The early interest of psychologists in stereotypes formed part of a broader concern with the origins of attitudes. They were interested in how attitudes changed and why some seemed more resistant to change than others. The stereotype was seen as an exceptional type of attitude – one that was particularly difficult to change. Thus the study of stereotype was closely linked to the notion of prejudice.

Prejudice implies an attitude that pre-judges reality and that is based not on experience but on some firmly fixed belief or dogma. The stereotype became the content of this belief, as it was projected on to particular persons or groups. As such, it revealed more of the individual – his/her beliefs and personality

– than the reality it described. It was a simple, negative and inaccurate image. Because it was so loosely related to the 'real world' it was not easily shifted by contrary evidence. The stereotype was seen as a rigid and unchanging attitude that was locked within the individual. Stereotypes were characteristically seen as expressions of hostility towards particular minority groups such as 'blacks' or 'Jews'. Stereotyped views were thought to be held by individuals who had little direct and personal experience of such groups.

The Authoritarian Personality (Adorno *et al.* 1950) is a good example of this approach. Here stereotyped attitudes towards subordinate minorities were explained as symptoms of a personality type that would project aggression on to the weak and the defenceless. As in this study, the psychological use of stereotypes was often motivated by political and humanitarian concerns such as the psychological roots of the 'fascist personality' and a concern with the fate of oppressed minorities. But the stereotyped views of the authoritarian person were still seen as a kind of personality disorder that was the result of a harsh and loveless childhood.

The sociological view of stereotypes

Sociologists want to look beyond the individual to see the part played by stereotypes in society. In particular they ask, who benefits from the stereotyping of certain groups? Prison warders, for example, often have a stereotyped view of prisoners as 'animals'. But such a perspective serves a purpose. It now becomes quite 'reasonable' to treat prisoners as less than human because that is 'just what they are'. Ideas and beliefs that are 'useful' in this way to those who hold them are what sociologists call ideologies – 'convenient' ideas that benefit some groups at the expense of others. Recent sociologists are particularly interested in the part played by stereotypes in ideologies.

Tessa Perkins (1979) argues that stereotypes, although simple in form, are in fact compressed and shorthand ways of referring to quite complex social relationships. Thus the 'dumb blonde' stereotype portrayed in many films refers to the subordinate position of women in western societies and in that sense is quite accurate. Women typically *do* find themselves in roles that are seen as less intellectually demanding. Women *are* often defined in terms of their physical attractiveness to men. But, as Richard Dyer (1977) argues, the stereotype goes further to suggest that such differences are inborn – they imply 'natural' differences between the sexes. It suggests, or reinforces, the view that women's social position is *caused by* differences in their aptitude and ability. In doing so it conceals the possibility that such differences may be the *effect* of their inferior position in a male dominated society. Thus it confuses cause and effect, and in doing so, serves the ideological function of making female disadvantage seem just, acceptable, and legitimate. The 'dumb blonde' stereotype is not, therefore, necessarily inaccurate, it reflects back the reality of women's exploited experience, but in doing so makes it seem inevitable and natural.

Perkins argues that stereotypes are not only held about minority groups of which we have little direct experience. To define them in this way limits their usefulness. Stereotypes of women (and men) are widespread yet few of us have no direct experience of the opposite sex. To see stereotypes as applying only to distant and alien minorities makes us blind to the ways in which they affect our everyday dealings with the people around us. For example, stereotypes which teachers hold about pupils are known to influence significantly how teachers treat pupils in the classroom. Even though we may not 'believe' the stereotype it remains as a part of our consciousness and works as a shorthand technique for conveying a complex idea.

Women

In the following discussion we will look at research into

stereotypes of women, gay men, and black people. As Gaye Tuchman says of the representation of women in American mass media:

'Relatively few women are portrayed there, although women are 51 per cent of the population and are well over 40 per cent of the labour force. Those working women who are portrayed are condemned. Others are trivialised as child-like adornments who need to be protected or they are dismissed to the protective confines of the home.'

(Tuchman 1981)

Summarizing television content analyses over a twenty-year period Tuchman shows that images of men outnumber those of women by two to one. If a working person is portrayed it is almost always a male image and those working women that are depicted are shown to be incompetent and inferior to male workers: 'men are doctors, women, nurses; men are lawyers, women secretaries; men work in corporations, women tend boutiques' (Tuchman 1981). Two thirds of the images of women shown on the screen are of women who have been, are, or are about to be, married. But the typical male image is of a single person.

These findings are rather crude measures of sex stereotyping in the media. They cannot catch the subtler points or the range of stereotypes of gender. There is not, for instance, one single stereotype of women but many: the 'mother-in-law', the 'secretary', the 'call-girl', etc.

Another danger of such content analyses is that they encourage an approach which views images and stereotypes as divorced from their wider social, political, and ideological contexts. Tuchman's own discussion of stereotypes in women's magazines shows that stereotypes are not static, they respond to changes in the actual position of women in society. Thus, in response to the growing women's movement and the increase in female employment, American women's magazines directed at working-class women displayed a more optimistic attitude towards the possibility of combining work and family responsibilities than did their predecessors, although a dominant ideology of femininity prevailed. Majorie Ferguson notes a similar shift in emphasis in a study of the three largest circulation women's magazines in Britain between 1949 and 1974 (Ferguson 1983). Unlike the earlier editions where love and marriage were the prime theme, this was displaced by the theme of self-development and individual achievement. In part, such shifts are dictated by commercial pressures in the highly competitive world of magazine journalism. In part, too, they represent attempts to re-work earlier ideologies into new forms, more in line with changing realities and beliefs, without challenging the overall subordination of women.

Gay men

Frank Pearce suggests that gay men, like women are 'the unspoken, denied a voice, a chance to express their own needs' in the mass media (Pearce 1981). The ideological basis for the presentation of gay men in the mass media is capitalist society's need for a clear distinction between the male and female role. 'Homosexual acts call into question the "natural" order which has been so necessary for industrial capitalism' (Pearce 1981: 315). Basing his research on newspaper reports of trials of homosexual men in Britain between 1952 and 1972 Pearce argues that the press have adopted a number of strategies to deal with male homosexuality.

One was simply to ignore the existence of such behaviour. Before 1950, he argues, homosexuals were almost never mentioned. Where they were depicted they were shown to be sub-human or 'sick', 'ill', or 'unfortunate'. Another strategy to resolve the threat to traditional gender roles was to question their masculinity – they were 'men with women's souls' (Pearce 1981: 308) and reports frequently stressed the 'feminity' of their appearance (concern with hair and dress) and occupation ('feminine' professions; window dressing, theatre, dress design, etc.). Stories of the homosexual coming to a 'bad end' were also used as an opportunity to reinforce conventional values. Like the public execution, such stories provided cautionary tales – a dramatic warning to those tempted to stray from approved paths.

Much of the power of the stereotype in media products is in its visual impact. Erving Goffman's (1979) analysis of visual images of men and women in advertising illustrates, in a convincing way, how gender roles are reproduced in the postures, relative positions, and expressions of men and women arranged by photographers and other image makers. That such images seem 'natural' to us is a strong reminder of the power of ideology to shape our thoughts without our conscious awareness. This 'hidden' effect of ideology makes the measurement and assessment of media effects through survey techniques suspect.

In the case of gay men visual imagery is frequently used as a kind of shorthand to 'establish' the gayness of the character. Dyer shows how the appearance, movement, and surroundings of gay characters in films are often set up to convey quickly their gayness (Dyer 1977: 32). A 'mincing' walk, jewellery, 'excessive' concern with stylish dress or furnishings frequently serve as signals of the sexual preference of the character. This is particularly important as gayness, unlike gender or 'colour', may not be immediately apparent.

Black people

A third area of stereotyping to have received considerable attention recently is that of stereotypes of black people. Hartmann and Husband's (1974) study of the contribution of the mass media to the formation of racial prejudice in the white population is of particular interest here. It is a widely quoted work which attempts to link stereotyped media images of 'coloured' people to a measurable change in the attitudes of white children. There is little research, using the concept of stereotype, that attempts to prove such a direct effect. Although more theoretically sophisticated than most of the effects research already mentioned it does not avoid all the pitfalls of the 'hypodermic' approach.

The 'cause' in Hartmann and Husband's research design was the way in which the mass media presented black people in terms of 'negative perceptions' and 'intergroup conflict'. This stereotyped image was discovered by a content analysis of race-related stories in four major British daily papers between 1963 and 1970. The 'effects' were measured by a survey of attitudes among children in schools with low and high numbers of 'coloured immigrant' children. They concluded that the 'interpretive frameworks' (ways of thinking) of the children fitted in with the dominant themes of the newspapers' reporting of race. The effects of the media were to encourage a concern with particular issues:

- The numbers of black people entering Britain.
- Hostility and discrimination between black people and whites.
- Laws to control immigration and discrimination.
- The views of the politican Enoch Powell.

They argue that:

> 'Children who live in areas of low immigration have to rely more heavily on the media for their information about coloured people than do others. Media-supplied information carries the suggestion of conflict more often than that from other sources. As a result these children are more prone to think about race relations in terms of conflict than are those in "high" contact areas, even though they (the "lows") live in places where the objective conditions for inter-group conflict are absent.'
>
> (Hartmann and Husband 1982)

Two reasons are suggested for the way in which the media report race. The first has its origins in the 'news values' of journalists (see pp. 94–9). Drawing on a study of foreign news by Galtung and Ruge (1981) they see news values as a kind of sixth sense that journalists acquire for what will make a 'good story'. Conflict, threat, and deviancy – dramatic and exciting events – make news, regardless of whether the subject is race or anything else. So do events that can be fitted into familiar frameworks 'existing images, stereotypes and expectations' (Hartmann and Husband 1981). One such framework was the reports of racial conflict in America during the 1960s.

The second reason is historical. In Chapter 2 of their book they describe the 'cultural legacy' of racism in Britain. 'Traditional images' of the black population can be traced back to colonialism and slavery in the eighteenth and nineteenth centuries, and further to medieval images of black symbolizing 'evil'. Such imagery is to be found elsewhere, in cartoon humour and children's books, as well as in news stories.

Reviewing the work of Hartmann and Husband, Andy Reeve and Paul Stubbs put forward a number of criticisms. The study fails, they argue, to explain the persistence of the ideology of racism and how it is related to current political and economic structures. Their emphasis on the role of news values leads to a neglect of ideological processes, the ways in which the mass media tend to reproduce 'the definitions of the powerful, of the dominant ideology' (Reeve and Stubbs 1981: 46).

Secondly their notion of the media audience (the children whose attitudes were measured) is, according to Reeves and Stubbs, oversimplified. Referring to the work of David Morley (see pp. 125–27 for a fuller account) and other recent work on youth subcultures such as Phil Cohen's (1972) article they argue that a much more detailed analysis of the audience is required, taking into account such factors as class, family, school, subcultural groups, and the history of the community. Finally a much more careful ideological analysis of the political scene is necessary that takes into account growing unemployment and its impact on black and white workers, changing laws to do with race, and the growth of black resistance.

However much of the work on which these criticisms are based was not available at the time Hartmann and Husband did their research. It retains a place as an important milestone in the development of our understanding of the effects of stereotypes.

Activity

Collect some examples of a particular stereotype from magazine advertisements and list the characteristics that are highlighted and appear regularly. The 'semantic differential' discussed later (p. 107) would be a useful method to use. Stereotypes of the elderly, or students would be interesting variations on those discussed above.

Further reading

There is a large literature on the stereotyping of women in the media: King and Stott (1977) and Adams and Laurikietis (1976) provide clear introductions. Dyer (1977) raises a number of interesting conceptual issues relating to stereotypes. See Holland (1981) for a revealing case study in the press treatment of black people (p. 98).

Agenda-setting – the ideological role of the mass media

In this section we examine some of the recent research into the effects of the media which shows how the media reproduce a dominant ideology. Marxist theory has made an important contribution to the development of this work, described by Stuart Hall as the 'critical' approach. The way in which ideas help the ruling class to retain their control over other groups and create consensus within society is an issue that has received a great deal of attention by modern Marxist writers. But even writers who would not place themselves within the Marxist tradition have recognized that the media and their effects cannot be studied in isolation from the other institutions and structures of society.

Neither is there complete agreement among Marxists concerning the existence of a dominant ideology which is expressed through the mass media. Criticism of the 'dominant ideology' approach has come both from within and outside the Marxist perspective. Marxist and pluralist critics have questioned whether there *is* a unified dominant ideology. They also point to cases where it appears that the media operate in ways that are in conflict with ruling class interests. But the research we shall now describe provides some of the most thorough attempts to overcome the problems of earlier work and to understand the role of the media in society.

The term 'agenda-setting' refers to a process whereby the terms of reference for debate are fixed to suit the interests of the powerful. It should be stressed that setting an agenda does not prohibit all debate or disagreement – it merely sets the boundaries within which the debate should take place. For example, imagine a teacher who sets up a debate with a group of pupils about why they failed an exam. The teacher lays down an agenda for this discussion which includes the following items: the 'laziness' of pupils, pupils not being intelligent enough to understand the syllabus, pupils being insufficiently motivated to succeed, and pupils receiving little encouragement at home. A wide-ranging discussion between the relative merits of these different 'causes' could then ensue, and perhaps some agreement might finally be reached on which was the main factor to be held responsible for the outcome. Such a teacher might well attempt to impress her or his colleagues with the 'democratic' relationship s/he had with the class.

To call such a discussion 'democratic' is obviously a fraud. A number of key issues would never be discussed because they were not included in the agenda. What about the quality of teaching, the shortage of textbooks, or the cramped conditions under which the class had to work? It may have been in the interests of the teacher and the school authorities to leave out such items, but we certainly cannot assume they had no bearing on the matter. And if the class were ultimately convinced that, whatever the correct explanation (laziness, stupidity, etc.), their poor results were in any case their own fault, then a subtle form of ideological control would have been successfully imposed on them.

It is in just such a way that the critical approach in media sociology sees the effects of the mass media. They provide an illusion of 'openness' as a forum for competing points of view, but this is all circumscribed within an overall 'discourse' or agenda which sets the limits to what shall and, more importantly, what shall *not*, be discussed by society.

Bad News – *television coverage of industrial disputes*

For example, the detailed research carried out in Britain by the Glasgow University Media Group (1976) seems to show that the mass media set an agenda for the discussion of these events which assumed that strikes were a threat to the 'national interest' (see pp. 104–07 for a discussion of their methods). Such an agenda sets up a discourse, an area for debate, within which certain items are permissible: is this strike a major or a minor threat to the 'national interest'? Should laws be introduced to limit the rights of workers to take industrial action or can we rely on their 'good will'? Other questions are ruled out of order: is it equally in the interests of employers *and* workers to ensure that production is not interrupted by disputes? Do workers have any other means at their disposal to defend themselves against attacks on their standard of living? If the agenda set by the mass media were fully accepted then the latter questions could not be posed at all by members of society. The fact that such questions do sometimes get raised shows that the ideological control of the media is not complete. For Marxists, the struggle between ruling classes and the working classes over ideology is just part of the wider conflict between the two groups which is rooted in economic

53

inequalities. In this struggle the mass media mainly reflect the interests of the dominant groups – the ruling-class ideology.

Further reading

Glasgow University Media Group (1982) provides an excellent readable summary of the main points of this research.

Welfare 'scroungers'

Another example of this approach is to be found in the work of Golding and Middleton (1982) on the presentation of the welfare claimant in the press. In the first part of their book they trace the history of the image of the poor from medieval times to the present day. Recurrent themes are: the belief that poverty is the product of idleness, that people 'ought' to work and be independent, and that help for the poor should always be closely monitored to ensure that it is not abused.

They then provide an account of a moral panic about social security fraud during the mid-1970s in the British media. The 'trigger' for the moral panic was the trial of an unemployed man in 1976 which produced extensive and 'hysterical' media coverage. Press accounts of the case stressed a number of related themes:

- The 'luxurious' lifestyle of the claimant.
- The 'generosity' of state benefits which were handed out without any regard to the 'real' needs of the claimant, or the interests of the taxpayer.
- The belief that this case was merely the 'tip of the iceberg' and that many similar cases had not yet come to light.
- The pressing need for politicians to take legislative action to prevent further fraud and to separate more effectively the 'scrounger' from the 'deserving poor'.

Content analysis of welfare stories over the period showed

that although welfare news usually occupied little space in the press there was a growth in the number of stories concerned with social security 'abuse'. Such stories frequently revived the themes of the 'idle poor' and the dangers of welfare abuse, an imagery that could be traced back to the middle ages: 'Underneath the acrid "scroungerphobia" of the late 1970s was the musty odour of the workhouse' (Golding and Middleton 1982). As in the cases of moral panic discussed earlier (pp. 36–42), official views received prominent treatment and little was heard of the views of claimants and the world as they perceived it. Little was heard, too, of the large sums of unclaimed benefits or the extent of tax fraud, both of which were much larger than estimated social security fraud.

In analysing the ideological context for the moral panic about 'scroungers', Golding and Middleton lay emphasis on a shift to the right of political opinion in response to the economic recession in Britain which had begun in the mid-1960s. Following Hall *et al.* (1978), they argue that the media reflect the interests of those in positions of power and privilege, who are the 'primary definers'. At a time of economic depression there occurred a reassertion of the 'basic values' of national unity, the work ethic, self-help, and traditional family life, and the welfare state was a major target of this new ideology. As one politician argued: 'The welfare state must be pruned in places, and pruning it will strengthen it like roses' (Golding and Middleton 1982). Such sentiments have been put into practice in recent welfare policies designed to encourage 'self-responsibility' and to provide 'the incentive of inequality' to the poor of the nation who were 'relaxing in the lap of welfare state luxury'.

'Law and order' and 'mugging'

The study by Stuart Hall and others (1978) of the politics of the 'law and order' panic concerning 'mugging' provides one of the most detailed ideological analyses of media effects. It gave an account of the origins of the moral panic, drawing on the 'deviancy amplification' concept. The threat of the 'mugger' served to justify and legitimate an escalation of social control – special 'anti-mugging' squads and excessive sentences on those convicted. But 'mugging' was a new label for a familiar group of offences. It provided an umbrella under which these were placed to create the impression of a rising tide of street violence.

The mass media were centrally involved in this process, faithfully reporting the statements and facts offered by the 'primary definers' – police spokespersons, judges and magistrates, and politicians. The views of these groups, played back to them through the media, are then taken as evidence of 'public opinion' and used as a mandate for further control. The media also 'fleshed out' the 'mugger' folk devil with stereotyped images of black youth in inner-city areas drawn from American media.

As in the 'scroungerphobia' described by Golding and Middleton, the moral panic concerning 'mugging' was initially focused around a key case. The 'defencelessness' of the victim (an elderly man), the 'irrationality' of the boys' behaviour (30 pence, a few keys, and five cigarettes were stolen), the severity of the attack (the boys returned to the scene of the crime to commit a second assault), and the racial background of the assailants (the boy who received the heaviest sentence, twenty years, was half West Indian, another was of Cypriot background), were all given heavy emphasis in the reports of the crime. These features provided the framework or 'inferential structure' for much of the reporting of 'similar' events that was to follow.

The 'law and order' campaign which ensued 'worked' because it preyed upon the fears, anxieties, and common-sense prejudices of the working class while at the same time providing a symbol around which 'consensus' and 'national unity' could be mobilized. The scapegoat of the 'mugger' was welcomed by a ruling class faced with increasing class divisions and bitterness. It was, in short, a solution to the 'ideological crisis'.

Each of the three studies mentioned in this section take as their background a crisis of control for capitalism in Britain during the 1970s. Each can be read as an aspect of the attempts by the state, through the services of the mass media, to respond to this crisis and reassert ideological control.

Within the 'critical' approach the media do have effects. The dominant ideology which they express, through words and images, is a major means by which the powerful secure their position. Like a dog on a long lead they offer the illusion of freedom which conceals the reality of constraint.

Further reading

The studies by Golding and Middleton (1982) and Hall et al. *(1978) are quite demanding. There is an Open University video by Stuart Hall ('Mugging') and a programme in the ITV 'Viewpoint' series ('The Welfare State') which summarize these works in an entertaining manner.*

3

The social context of media production

This chapter looks at the organizations which make up the mass media: the television companies, newspapers, radio stations, and publishers. As we have seen, earlier media researchers were mainly concerned with the media product and its effects on audiences. Such researchers showed little curiosity about the origins of media messages. But if, as many recent studies suggest, the mass media spread ideas that are misleading, distorted, untrue, one-sided, or sensationalized, then the organizations that produce these messages become a natural object of enquiry. Cohen and Young (1981) go so far as to argue that further research into effects should cease until more is understood about the organizations that produce the mass media.

This is, of course, an ambitious goal. Media organizations are complex and varied. They take different forms in different countries. In some places the state seems to monopolize mass media production, using it as an instrument of government. In other countries the 'freedom' of the press is spoken of in tones of reverence. Most mass media are in the hands of big companies and are subject to the same sort of influences as any other capitalist enterprise. Mass media are industries which make use of some of the most advanced technology yet devised and the rate of technological innovation in this field is increasing rapidly. Some writers predict that the development of information technology will have consequences as far-reaching as those of the industrial revolution.

Figure 1. Influences on media organizations

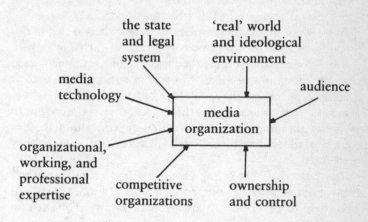

The diagram above attempts to map out simply the main influences on media organizations.

Activity

Take a large sheet of paper and as you read this chapter try to fill in some of the details of the relationships between the various influences on media organizations. If you do this thoroughly your diagram will be much more complicated (but also much more useful!) than the one above.

Theoretical considerations

Before we go on to look in detail at the organizations which make up the mass media, it will be useful to consider briefly some different viewpoints on society that lie behind the work of many sociologists – including those who study the media.

One approach which has been a strong influence on media sociologists in recent years is based on the work of Karl Marx. Writing before the development of TV, film, and radio, Marx did produce a number of useful insights into the role of the media in capitalist societies. His own experience as a journalist was a useful resource in this (see Murdock 1982).

In his view, all capitalist societies were split into two major sections. A small group of powerful people (the ruling class), through their ownership of the factories and equipment used to make the things needed by people in society, were able to dominate all other groups. These other groups, to whom Marx referred collectively as the working classes, were put to work by the dominant group as employees, although they were not allowed to receive the full value of the work they performed.

The power of this ruling group or class arose from their control of the economy but, according to Marx, it spread out from here to cover all other aspects of society. For such an unequal system to persist it was essential that the exploited working classes were kept under firm control. At its most basic level this was achieved through the power that owners had to sack workers and deny them the means of earning their living, but this control extended throughout the major institutions of society: church, school, family, and the state itself. For Marx, the state was no neutral institution which represented in a democratic way the interests of all. Regardless of the electoral processes that led to the selection of a government, the state, in a capitalist society, would continue to represent, in the main, the interests of the ruling class. For these reasons, he believed, it was impossible to change society gradually through democratic elections.

The control of the ruling classes extended also into the control of ideas. 'In every historical epoch', wrote Marx, 'the dominant ideas are those of the dominant class.' The mass media are to be included in this observation. It is to be expected, from a Marxist perspective, that the dominant ideas that they express will reflect ruling-class interests.

Commercial influences

Media organizations can be subjected to a variety of commercial influences. In the west the majority of media organizations are themselves commercial undertakings. They are usually part of some bigger industrial or financial group. In either case the need to maintain profitability is likely to be an influence on their activities. As we shall see there is debate among sociologists about the extent to which profit-seeking is the prime motive in large modern corporations (see pp. 64–7).

For many of the media organizations advertising is an important, and sometimes the most important, source of revenue. Consequently the requirements of advertisers have been a significant influence on the content and development of the media.

Not all media organizations are in private ownership. Many are part of the public sector, sponsored and regulated by the state, where the main requirement is to provide a public service: informing, educating, and entertaining audiences. The BBC in Britain and the French RTF (Radio-telediffusion française) are examples of such organizations. There is discussion among media sociologists about whether such arrangements leave the organization free from government and commercial influence (see pp. 69–78). They nevertheless have to exist within a commercial environment and their performance is often assessed by commercial criteria. Often they engage directly in commercial activities. The BBC supplements its revenue from licence fees by the sale of books and recordings to the general public and of TV programmes to broadcasting organizations in other countries.

The development of the British press

Historical accounts of the British press often portray its development as a heroic struggle for political and economic independence (Williams 1965). Many authors agree that the middle of the nineteenth century was an important watershed in the development of a 'free' press (see pp. 69–71 for further discussion of this concept). They argue that the growth of advertising revenue freed the newspapers from financial dependence on political parties and the government.

Other accounts (e.g. Curran and Seaton 1981) suggest that this version of events is merely an ideology that serves to justify and legitimate the past and present role of advertising. In this view, the growth of advertising brings not freedom but a new form of constraint – the substitution of one form of control by another, less visible but more efficient and self-sustaining: the market.

> 'Market forces succeeded where legal repression had failed in establishing the press as an instrument of social control, with lasting consequences for the development of modern British society.'
>
> (Curran 1977)

In the nineteenth century Britain had a radical press which was able to focus on its working-class audience. It was a mouthpiece for the interests and concerns of this group. It was politically committed and critical of society. It maintained close links with its audience – many of whom were also contributors. In the early days of the British press it was possible to set up a newspaper with very limited capital. For £10 a hand press could be acquired, metal type could be hired, and print workers paid on a casual basis. Distribution and sales of radical newspapers were carried out by volunteers. Unlike the modern newspaper, costs were covered by sales revenue. Curran argues that this independent press was effectively destroyed by the growth in advertising.

The influence of advertisers worked in two ways. Some

papers that supported radical, anti-capitalist causes were boycotted by advertisers and thus forced to close. Direct action of this type was much less common than the second, less visible influence. In seeking the patronage of advertisers, popular working-class newspapers were encouraged to broaden their readership. An exclusively working-class audience had little appeal for advertisers.

From the advertisers' perspective, the ideal publication is that which puts their product before the audience that is most likely to buy it. Newspapers which have a large middle-class readership are thus in a privileged position. The nineteenth-century popular working-class press was forced to modify its content to appeal to a broad cross-section of society or become a small circulation journal supported by subscription. No longer could mass circulation papers *afford* to reflect exclusively the interests of working-class audiences.

As a result of such influences, the successful mass circulation newspapers of the twentieth century are those that have abandoned a committed radical style of reporting, with priority given to political news, international news, and social comment. These have been replaced by sport, 'human interest' stories ('ABANDONED PUPPY SAVED BY ANIMAL-LOVING GRANNY'), and sensationalism ('TEENAGE POP IDOL DRUGS SHOCK').

The influence of advertisers is not, of course, restricted to the press. Barnouw (1978) has shown how American TV drama producers after the Second World War were encouraged by advertisers to stop making plays about working-class life. This was not because they were unpopular – indeed they had high audience ratings – but because advertisers felt that such programmes did not provide the right sort of settings for their products. Instead they promoted adventure/action series:

'Drama moved outdoors into active glamorous settings. Handsome heroes and heroines set the tone – and some proved willing to do commercials, and even appear at sales meetings and become company spokesmen.'

(Barnouw 1978)

63

The 'managerial revolution': a softening of capitalism?

An alternative to Curran's Marxist history of the British press is the view of some sociologists that the changing forms of capitalism have transformed and democratized all industrial organizations including the mass media. According to this view, which developed around the middle of the twentieth century, Marxist analysis of economic life as a system of exploitation is outmoded. Modern corporations no longer make the single-minded pursuit of profit their prime goal. Instead the swollen strata of corporate managers, technologists, and professionals that characterize the modern company run their organizations in a humane and socially responsible way.

There are two main strands to this argument. The first is the growth of a new sort of capitalist enterprise: the joint stock company. The crucial watershed in this 'shift in the nature of capitalism' was the change in company law which allowed outside investors to buy shares in a company. It is certainly true that few large companies are now owned by just one individual or family. An ever-increasing demand for capital has drawn in a large and diverse group of investors who lack the unity and decisiveness of a single owner. It is argued that the owners of modern corporations do not make up a cohesive social group which can act together to manage the day-to-day business of the company. Instead, the modern corporation is controlled by a group of professional managers who are not motivated exclusively by profit.

The second main strand of the argument is that company growth during the twentieth century has reinforced the power of the manager. As enterprises have become larger and more complex they demand greater technological expertise. No longer can one individual, or even group, hope to keep complete overall control of the diverse range of activities of such an organization. Therefore, it is argued, the interests of the owners – the 'naked pursuit of profit' – no longer has first priority. As power is taken up by managers, administrators, and technologists, other goals are said to rise to the surface: a concern with the interests of customers (the audience in the case of the media) and employees, with producing a high quality product, with professional integrity, and with company expansion.

This view of industrial development has not lacked critics. How useful is it as a picture of the development of the communications industry?

The growth of the multinational media conglomerate

Certainly the scale of media organizations has increased dramatically – so too has the level of technology involved. High-speed printing presses, computerized techniques of composing and laying out pages, colour television, international communications satellites, etc. are technologies which have revolutionized the means of mass communication. Large numbers of skilled professionals are needed to operate and administer these vast technologically advanced industries. Massive investment is required to sustain this growth. Media industries, like many others, have sought the support of outside investors to provide the necessary capital.

Small shareholders

The first main strand of the argument is correct in its claim that small shareholders are now much more numerous. The ownership of the Associated Communications Corporation (ACC is the parent company of ATV Network), for example, is shared among thirteen thousand separate investors, most of whom have holdings of less than one thousand units. But it is wrong to assume that this has led to a shift of power from owners to managers.

There are two reasons for this. Firstly, in most companies there are a few substantial shareholders who are able to dominate company meetings. Founder and current chairman Sir Lew Grade and his two managing directors of ACC have between them over 50 per cent of the shares, which enables

65

them to outvote all the other shareholders. Five of the top seven companies that control the British national press are controlled by the descendants of the original founding families and their associates. In America Columbia pictures and CBS Inc. are under the control of their proprietors.

Secondly, small shareholders have very little individual voting power and are unlikely to organize collectively to overthrow large shareholders. Most take little interest in the management of the company and rarely attend meetings. Consequently it is very easy for a few well-organized substantial shareholders to take effective control of a company – sometimes as little as 5 per cent of shares is enough.

The second main strand of the argument is that companies are now too large and complex to be run from the top so that power devolves to managers, administrators, and professional experts. Certainly as media organizations grow in size company owners cannot keep track of the day-to-day details of every part of the company organization. They lack the time and expertise to maintain detailed operational control. But through the board of directors they retain the power to make the big decisions about company goals and policies, whether and in what direction growth should occur, how much of the profits should be distributed and how much ploughed back into the business. This kind of control has been dubbed 'allocative' control by Pahl and Winkler (1974). The effective owners (large shareholders) are able to set the general framework within which managers and professional employees operate. Within these boundaries employees may have considerable leeway, artistic and editorial 'freedom' – the freedom to decide the best way to use given resources to achieve the goals set for them by the organization – but only so long as they continue to comply with the owners' wishes.

Conglomerates

As companies have increased in size they have decreased in number. In many industrial sectors a few companies dominate the market-place – and media industries are no exception:

> 'half the commercial TV programmes that are transmitted, over two-thirds of paperback and record sales, over three-quarters of women's magazine circulation, and over nine-tenths of national daily and Sunday paper circulation, are controlled by the five leading companies in each sector.'
>
> (Curran and Seaton 1981)

Most of the big media companies have *diversified* into related industry sectors – a company that started out in newspapers, for example, may take a stake in a new TV or commercial radio company. Many too have spread their net further afield by buying up companies that are not connected with the media. Such enterprises are known as conglomerates – an assorted mixture of companies whose business may cover a wide range of products and services. Where such growth involves the purchase of or by foreign companies the result is a *multinational conglomerate*. Massive corporations of this sort are now a feature of modern capitalism. In many cases they wield more economic power than some of the poorer nation states of the world.

This sort of development from the point of view of the media conglomerate, is clearly a sensible strategy for corporate growth. Diversified companies are guarding against risk by not putting all their eggs into one basket. The overall profitability of the conglomerate does not depend on the success of any one industry or, if multinational, any one country. Resources can be transferred around the different component companies in response to state regulations and in the pursuit of maximum profits. The growth in the scale of companies squeezes out effective companies which might otherwise hinder the growth of profits.

Activity

It is difficult to trace the complex web of ownership and control of large multinationals. They often have shares in each other's companies (interlocking shareholdings) and their involvement is often hidden by operating through a differently named subsidiary or sometimes a chain of subsidiary companies. Like many powerful groups they do not welcome the scrutiny of sociologists.

You may be able to discover for yourself some evidence of the concentration of ownership by looking through a particular branch of the media (e.g. women's magazines or children's comics, etc.) and making a list of who publishes them. You could do a much more thorough job by using *Willings Press Guide*, available in most public libraries, which lists all newspapers and periodicals in Britain with their publishers and circulations.

Do commercial influences have any effect?

It has been argued that commercial influences such as those described in this section are not important because it is the consumer who calls the tune. The owners of companies are in business to make a profit and this can only be achieved by giving the public what it wants.

But as we have seen in the case of the British press it is the advertisers not the audience who are the 'real' customers for newspapers and who have a major effect on the content of the media. There is evidence, too, that owners can and do exert direct control in certain circumstances, as the following extract from an interview with one proprietor, Sir James Goldsmith, illustrates:

'Interviewer: If the editor and you disagree, what do you do?
Goldsmith: It's the same as in any other business. If you disagree with the editor, it's give and take – and sometimes you give in, sometimes he gives in. If a disagreement becomes such that you can't live together, then the editor goes, just like a managing director would.'

(quoted in Murdock 1982)

But such direct control is a last resort. The most effective control exerted by owners is indirect. Company employees know that in order to succeed and be promoted they must comply with the goals laid down for them and avoid contentious material that might give offence to the owners. These boundaries become the common-sense assumptions of the organization which are rarely questioned.

When the media organization is just one part of a multinational conglomerate there may be, within the organization, a diverse range of constituent companies whose interests must be taken into account. Richard Bunce (1976) has linked the production of a documentary on urban mass transportation systems by the American TV company WBC to the fact that its parent company (Westinghouse Electric) was the main supplier of such systems.

He has also suggested that a documentary critical of the American involvement in the Vietnam war was turned down by the three main TV networks because their parent companies were all involved in servicing the war effort (examples cited in Murdock 1982).

Activity

Imagine that you have just written a TV script which depicts graphically the horrors of nuclear war. You wish to sell this play to a TV company which you discover is part of a multinational corporation, one part of which is engaged in arms manufacture. Try to think of some of the arguments you might try to present to convince the company that your play should be produced by them.

The media and the state

The freedom of the press

In the west the freedom to publish is frequently regarded as one of the sacred values of democracy alongside free speech and freedom of opinion. The freedom to publish is not merely a protection for the individual from the excesses of government; it is seen as a cornerstone of democracy and thus of benefit to society as a whole.

This flattering view of the role of the mass media is widely embraced by writers, journalists, and broadcasters. They make up what is sometimes described as the 'fourth estate' (the others being the government, the judiciary, and the church), whose role is to seek out corruption and stand up for the rights of the ordinary people:

> 'muck-rakers, gadflies, cross examiners of the great on behalf of the common people, convenors of public debate and conveyors of hard fact . . . they help to keep liberal democracy alive in societies too populous and too complex for face-to-face exchange to suffice.'
>
> (Westergaard 1977)

Included in this notion of a 'free' press is the idea that between them the media express a range of views that satisfy the tastes and opinions of all. The free press idea is an important component of the pluralist view of politics, in which power is balanced between competing groups and interests but where no one group is dominant. Such freedom is often contrasted with the position of the press in countries like the Soviet Union where it is seen to be more a lap-dog of the state than a watchdog of the people.

The view of the press as watchdog is criticized by Cirino (1973). Many matters of importance to the public are effectively suppressed in the media by powerful interest groups. Issues like the scale of hunger and malnutrition among America's poor, the hazards of motor vehicle design, and the dangers of smoking – issues uncomfortable for politicians and large corporations – are systematically excluded from media coverage. Rarely, he claims, do the media *lead* a campaign of protest, although they may be forced to adopt it once it is firmly established.

The reality of state intervention

But how valid is the claim that the media in western democracies are an independent force – one of the guarantors of liberty? The details of the relationship between the state and the media will, of course, vary with time and place. But the freedom of the press is to a large extent a myth – a myth that is nevertheless much cherished by governments for the image of democracy that it confers. In practice no government, be it 'democratic' or 'totalitarian', has allowed the mass media to develop unfettered by some form of regulation and control. The mass media have too powerful an influence on citizens to allow them unlicensed freedom. One of the clearest indications of this is the way in which invading forces now make the capture of the media (especially radio and television stations) a priority goal.

But a desire to maintain the myth of the 'free' press does force governments to act with circumspection when dealing with the media. Despite the reality of intervention, governments prefer not to be seen to be interfering with the freedom of the press. Thus control is often disguised; it is made to operate indirectly through semi-autonomous bodies or, most effectively, through mechanisms of self-regulation. There is no need to 'police' a mass medium that is itself so well-disciplined that it never steps out of line. The arsenal of powers that the state is able to deploy against the media is for the most part kept in reserve – a deterrent to deviance and a spur to self-control.

National emergencies

During periods of crisis and 'national emergency', governments are likely to resort to more direct forms of control over the media. For example governments frequently possess contingency arrangements for the control of the media during wartime.

At the beginning of the Second World War the British

coalition government led by Winston Churchill banned, for a time, the communist *Daily Worker* newspaper on the grounds that it was a threat to a unified war effort, and the much larger circulation *Daily Mirror* was threatened with similar treatment. In both these cases it has been argued (Curran and Seaton 1981) that the real motive for suppression was to muzzle political criticism rather than to protect national security.

The BBC and the Second World War

The 1939–45 war was an important time for the BBC, during which it grew considerably in size and public recognition. It was also a period during which the relationship between the BBC and the state was more firmly established.

During the General Strike of 1926, moves were made to commandeer the corporation. But this concession was won by offering general support to the government. Reith argued that 'since the BBC was a national institution and since the Government in this crisis was acting for the people ... the BBC was for the Government in the crisis too' (quoted in Curran and Seaton 1981).

However, the BBC refused to engage in crude anti-strike propaganda as Curran concludes: 'the General Strike marks the end of propaganda based on lies and the start of a more subtle tradition of selection and presentation' (Curran and Seaton 1981).

At the start of the Second World War there were those in the government, as in 1926, who wished to take over the BBC – but, as before, the corporation resisted. It was argued that to be effective the BBC had to be believed. It would have more credibility at home and abroad as an independent organization than as the puppet of the government. However, the government retained indirect influence. Through the Ministry of Information it provided much of the factual material on which news stories were based. But the corporation did not, on the whole, broadcast straightforward lies – defeats were not magically transformed into victories. In this case the truth may have been the best propaganda for an extended and sustained war effort.

The BBC was obliged to change to attract a wider audience. Two channels were offered: a 'Forces Network' featuring popular music and a 'Home Service' with a stress on talks, news, drama, and information. Staff numbers trebled and a new, more popular style was developed. Newsreaders, no longer anonymous Oxbridge-accented voices, announced their names at the start of the broadcast and spoke with regional accents. News reporters developed a style based on the pace and enthusiasm of sports reports, carefully avoiding complex language. The BBC established an image that served to unite the population because it overlooked some of the grimmer realities of the war.

The BBC's 'responsible' handling of sensitive political issues that arise during such national emergencies has earned it a degree of autonomy from the state. But this is not a bargain between equal partners. Like the trusted prisoner, good behaviour may win certain privileges but the stubborn facts of imprisonment remain.

More recently the war in the South Atlantic between Britain and Argentina over the sovereignty of the Malvinas/Falkland Islands led the British government to censor directly the stories that journalists on board the British task force were able to send back to the British press. After the war journalists complained that military censors had refused material on grounds of style and taste as well as for legitimate military reasons. Even references to the fact that reports had been subject to military censorship were censored. The government was also accused of being unco-operative in facilitating the transmission of television pictures of the conflict back to British viewers. Through direct censorship, delays in clearance for 'controversial' stories, and its control of communications media (especially communications satellites) the government maintained a very effective direct control over what the British media reported about the war (see Harris 1983).

Control of information – state secrets

'When the State is in danger, our own cherished freedoms, and even the rules of natural justice have to take second place.'

(Lord Denning)

In the modern state journalists and reporters are highly dependent on information provided for them by the government. Control over this information flow provides governments with an important means of influencing the media.

The Official Secrets Act

A major mechanism for this control is the classification of information as state secrets. The British government, for example, surrounds its activities with one of the most inpenetrable blankets of secrecy to be found in the West. This is the much-criticized Official Secrets Act, signed by two million British civil servants, which assumes every official activity to be an official secret unless otherwise designated by a civil servant. The all-embracing nature of this law was neatly expressed by Sir Martin James-Furnival, former head of the intelligence department MI5: 'It's an official secret if it's in an official file'.

The Act has often been used by British governments to silence their critics. A breach of the Act is committed if a civil servant discloses, or a member of the public knowingly receives, an official secret. Junior civil servant Sarah Tisdall was sent to jail in 1984 for passing on information to the *Guardian* newspaper about the manipulation of Parliament by the Defence Minister Michael Heseltine.

The 'hunger' of journalists 'starved' of information by state secrecy creates another mechanism for manipulating the media – the government 'leak'. These are frequently not genuine 'leaks' but 'controlled releases' of information that the government wishes to become more widely known. Among the public relations sections of government departments this has become a recognized method of news management – an essential part of the negotiated agreement between journalists and government information officers.

D (Defence)–Notices

'You think we lie to you. But we don't lie, really we don't. However when you discover that, you make an even greater error. You think we tell you the truth.'
(comment attributed to a senior British Civil servant, quoted in Chibnall 1977)

The D-Notice is a good example of the way in which the government can control the press by informal means. The D-Notice is the means by which members of the press are 'advised' of areas of government activity not open to public scrutiny in the media. Although journalists are not required by law to abide by these recommendations it is certainly in their long-term interest to do so. 'Disobedient' reporters may well find that an important source of information about government activities has been lost. As Aubrey (1981) suggests, the government maintains a very effective control over reporters by means of the 'stick' of the law and the 'carrot' of access to inside sources of information – for those reporters who have not incurred the displeasure of the government.

Crime reporters and the police

In many areas of journalism the reporter has to rely on a particular organization for information. The crime reporter, for example, cannot function without the co-operation of the police. Recently media sociologists have come to recognize that the relationship a journalist has with such official sources may strongly affect the stories that are written. It is one of the subtle means by which the state, as a major source of information, can control what the media report.

It has been alleged, for example, that following a series of conflicts between the police and young people in a number of British cities in 1981 (the 'riots'), the police have refused to tell the press when similar events have since occurred. Whatever their reasons, this shows that the police can and do suppress stories about which there is great public interest and concern.

Steve Chibnall's (1977) analysis of crime reporting in the British press illustrates this. A reciprocal relationship develops, one that benefits both the police and the reporter. The journalist can become a source of information for the police, in particular from the criminal underworld. Similarly the police can use the crime reporter to appeal to the public for information on, or witnesses to, a crime. False or misleading information may be released in order to hoax a criminal into feeling secure from detection or to panic him into making a mistake which leads to capture. In other cases stories may be created as a smokescreen to draw the attention of the public away from some other 'sensitive' aspect of police activity.

The crime reporter is, of course, often aware that these news management techniques are being used by police spokespeople. But failure to co-operate with the police will make the journalist's job much more difficult, if not impossible.

The police have a number of methods to ensure that the media are 'helpful'. Journalists who produce stories critical of the police are likely to be 'frozen-out'. They will receive no assistance from the police in their stories. But this often only produces more 'hostile' stories, and the journalist who is punished in this way will anyway be able to obtain information from other journalists. More effective is the technique Chibnall calls 'buttering-up'. Drinks, lunches, and exclusive stories may be offered as inducements to toe the line. Reporters who remain critical may be harassed directly by the police – followed, questioned, and threatened with arrest. The same techniques are used by army press officers with journalists who cover events in Northern Ireland.

It is no coincidence, claims Chibnall, that these techniques have been developed at a time when there has been a growth in politically motivated crime ('terrorism') and prosecutions for police corruption. The police hold fairly specific models to explain both phenomena: 'terrorists' are vicious criminals who lack even the justification of greed, while corrupt police officers are the exceptional 'bad apple' in an otherwise good barrel. The media, on the whole, faithfully reproduce these versions of events.

Libel

Laws of libel exist to protect individuals against unjustified or damaging public statements. As such they are an important legal safeguard of the citizen's right to personal privacy – one supported by many international bodies such as the European Convention. This law can be in conflict with the activity of investigative journalism – the interpretation of libel in the USA, for instance, allows much more freedom to the press than in Britain.

The most serious criticism of the working of the law in Britain is that it provides protection only for the rich and powerful. Libel cases are very expensive and losers may have to pay the legal costs of both parties. Legal aid – a system of financial support for the legal costs of the poor – is not available for such actions in Britain. In effect this means that most ordinary people cannot afford the financial risk of a legal action against a national newspaper, for example, even where they have a strong case. The law also inhibits journalists in what they write about the wealthy, for they too may not be able to afford a legal action brought by a wealthy plaintiff, however sound their defence.

But the law of libel may be a two-edged sword, even in the hands of the powerful. Curran (1977) has shown that the use by government of this law against the emerging popular working-class radical press in Britain was counter-productive. Juries seemed unwilling to convict in such cases. But more importantly, even those cases the government won served only to boost the circulation of the journal concerned. The government turned instead to a system of taxes on newspapers, their advertisements, and newsprint (the paper on which they were printed) in an attempt to price working-class readers and publishers out of the market.

Contempt of court

This law constrains what reporters may say about court cases that have begun or are about to. It is an important protection of the right of the individual to a fair trial. The US version of this law gives much more freedom to the press and allows, for example, interviews with witnesses and reconstructions of cases before the trial has begun. But the law of contempt has sometimes served to 'muzzle' investigative journalism by banning the publication of stories of general public interest that are the subject of court proceedings.

A famous case of this was the ban on an article that was to have been published in the *Sunday Times* in Britain. It had alleged negligence on the part of the Distillers Company, makers of the drug Thalidomide. The article was ruled in contempt of court because of its possible effect on the outcome of cases against the company due to be brought on behalf of the children affected by the drug. It has been argued that the revised 1981 Contempt of Court Act, although allowing more room for press comment on court cases, would not have protected the *Sunday Times* in an equivalent situation today (Wallington 1984).

Public service broadcasting and the market-place

Two competing views have shaped the political and academic discussion of broadcasting. One sees broadcasting as a public service not concerned with profit. The other holds that the interests of the audience are best served if broadcasting organizations are commercial enterprises.

In practice both systems have coexisted in most countries. Commercial broadcasting was introduced into Britain (TV in 1956, radio in 1973), and even the US, home of the commercial broadcasting free-for-all, has its public service channels. However, the state has not relinquished an interest in broadcasting even in those countries where the commercial ethos reins supreme. In every country the state has attempted to regulate broadcasting in some way by allocating frequencies to stations, and frequently attempting to ensure that no one group of companies gains a monopoly.

In recent years the balance of arguments between the two competing views has shifted towards the commercial model. Collins (1983a) suggests two reasons for this. First there has been an ideological shift towards views that are increasingly critical of notions of public service, state control, and intervention. This has been associated with a strong swing to the right in British and American politics. The second reason is the fact that new methods have been developed for broadcasting signals which overcome the technical limitations of conventional broadcasting. Direct broadcasting by satellite and a new generation of cables which allow a broad range of bands to be transmitted down them, mean that it is now possible to transmit an almost unrestricted range of choices for consumers.

These services offer the potential of being increasingly interactive rather than simply one-way processes of communication. They are expected to revolutionize patterns of work (which may now be done from home) and consumption (shopping by direct order from home). The support given to these developments by many governments is based on the optimistic belief that by nurturing the development of these new technologies they will create the conditions for a new industrial revolution which will generate an economic revival both nationally and internationally.

Two examples will be examined here. The case of French broadcasting is interesting because until recently it was a total state monopoly. By contrast the development of broadcasting in the USA has always embraced enthusiastically the commercial model and has in recent years moved to a policy of almost complete non-intervention by the state. The US case is particularly relevant because it is so often cited as an example for emulation by other countries.

State-controlled broadcasting: the French case

The French Revolution was the source of many of the liberal ideals on which the notion of a free press is based. Yet French media have in fact been subject to the most stringent government controls; they are 'the most disciplined media in Europe' (Raboy 1983).

The French state has monopolistic control over Agence France Press (AFP), one of the big four international news agencies which supply international news stories to the world's leading news organizations. Through AFP it is involved in the production and distribution of information. It also owns the country's most important advertising agency (for the significance of this see pp. 61–3) and a total monopoly (until 1982) on electronic media and their development – including broadcast radio and television.

The French broadcasting authority Radio-telediffusion française (RTF) was under direct government control, and news programming was daily scrutinized and vetted by a succession of Ministers of Information. In effect, public broadcasting became merely a channel for the expression of government policy: 'Opposition politicians had no access to the air while the President and members of his government had unlimited access' (Raboy 1983). It was also unresponsive to young and minority audiences.

By contrast, the written press in France showed an unusually wide diversity of political opinion. This was paradoxically the result of another state monopoly – on the distribution of newspapers and journals. Nevertheless dissatisfaction with pro-government broadcasting grew from the mid-1970s – most noticeably with the emergence of hundreds of pirate radio stations (*radio libres*) broadcasting alternative political views.

In 1982 the new socialist government under President Mitterrand gave up the government monopoly on broadcasting, allowing local community radio stations to be set up. It broke the links between the government and national radio and television by creating an intermediate body (the *Haute Autorité*) modelled on the lines of the British Broadcasting Corporation (BBC) but having responsibility over all the media, state and private, radio, television, cable, and satellite.

This has led to much more diversity in French radio. Paris, for example, now has a choice of twenty-one radio stations catering for different cultural and political tastes. *Frequence Gaie* is a twenty-four-hour station for lesbians and gays. Others cater for different musical tastes; folk, pop, classical.

This cultural and political diversity is threatened by the financial problems of many of the new stations. The government gives them a small grant (£3,000 per year) not really sufficient for long-term stability and has since yielded to pressure and permitted stations to take advertising. This exposes them to commercial pressures – the need to appeal to the sort of audience advertisers prefer (see section on commercial influences). It also makes concentration more likely. One or two companies rise to pre-eminence and squeeze smaller competitors out. Bypassing regulations which prohibit this, *Radio NRJ* has established a network of twenty-three radio stations across the country. Italy, which opened broadcasting to local access in the mid-1970s without the French safeguards against monopoly control, now has a rich media entrepreneur, Silvio Belasconi, operating three private television networks with a daily audience of twelve million and 80 per cent of TV advertising.

Even the best-intentioned government action to broaden access to broadcasting can go wrong. It is crucial that commercial interests are rigorously contained or alternative sources of finance found if broadcasting diversity is to be possible.

'Free market broadcasting' – the US case

Although in America broadcasting has grown largely under commercial control the state has been active from the earliest days (Streeter 1983). The agency through which the state attempted to regulate broadcasting was the Federal Communications Commission (FCC). The current structure of US broadcasting was established in 1924 when four major companies sat down together to carve up the broadcasting market. The government gave its support to this division. In so doing it set up the conditions for the further growth of private monopolies. To appease public concern the FCC was established to regulate broadcasting, to guarantee free competition, and to represent the public interest.

US broadcasting policy, expressed through the FCC, is based on two assumptions. The first is the belief that free, impersonal market forces will produce competition between rival broadcasting companies – all public complaints to the FCC about broadcasting have been narrowly interpreted in terms of there not being enough competition. Second, it is assumed that such competition, if it can be arranged, will be in the best interests of the audience. Streeter argues that the effect of competition has often been to reduce rather than enhance the amount of choice for audiences. The need to generate large audiences for advertisers results in standardized programmes, written to formulae that have been successful in the past, or to copying the successful programmes of competitors.

Given these assumptions, US policy was, in fact, inconsistent. Far from encouraging competition, it gave its seal of approval to the domination of broadcasting by a few companies (oligopoly). It forced the existing companies to stop the 'unfair practices' which prevented the entry of new companies to broadcasting, but it did not recognize that the older companies were sufficiently well established to squeeze out new competitors.

Streeter explains these inconsistencies by arguing that the FCC's role has been ritualistic. Its role is to convince people that something is being done. It has been ineffective in curbing the power and influence of the giant media corporations but it has been effective in going through the *motions* of taking on the corporations, thus producing 'the satisfying spectacle of a successful challenge to the networks, complete with aggressive inquiries, public tribunals, and condemnations of the self-serving actions of wealthy and powerful business executives' (Streeter 1983). But it is only the illusion and not the reality of a challenge to the corporations; it allays public fears and suspicions while continuing to further the interests of the corporations it is supposed to be regulating.

The most recent response of the state has been to support the view of the broadcast companies that state intervention is not effective in securing competition. The 1980 *FCC Final Report on New Television Networks* argues that regulation does not work and that a new policy of *de*-regulation would be most effective. This overlooks the fact that the whole trend of broadcasting development in the USA is towards the development of an oligopoly. It also overlooks the possibility of reducing the power of the commercial corporations by developing public service broadcasting. As Streeter remarks, the only successful challenge to this oligopoly has come from the new public broadcasting system.

A key element that underwrites the faith of the FCC in de-regulation as a policy is a faith in the new communications technologies which promise the consumer increased choice from a diversity of specialized programmes. But, Streeter argues, why should new technologies open up choice? In America the commercial companies have yet not taken up all their options on existing UHF broadcast frequencies – there are still unused channels. This is because broadcasters do not feel the market exists for further channels to be developed profitably.

The media and technological change

Most of the familiar forms of the mass media have developed within the lifetime of one individual. Many more changes, involving new cable links, computers, and satellites, are under way or in prospect. So it is not surprising that people ask: what changes have technology brought about? What effects will it have in the future?

Technological determinism – a cautionary note

For sociologists, such questions have to be regarded with caution. The danger they sense in them is that of an oversimplified and unbalanced view of social change in which technology takes the leading role. Put simply, it suggests that social change occurs in the following ways: someone thinks of a new technique; everyone else says 'What a good idea!' and starts using it; and social life is never quite the same again.

There are many examples of such thinking in accounts of social change. New inventions and technical ideas are seen to have an inevitable and determining effect on society. Hence, this view of social change has become known as *technological determinism*. It is a view that has been particularly prevalent in histories of the mass media, partly because its technologies have been changing so fast.

What is wrong with this view? Certainly technology has an important effect on our lives, but to suggest that it determines how we live can easily be shown to be wrong. If you are given a gun you *can* kill other people; but you don't *have to*. How you act will depend on the social circumstances in which you find yourself. Technology *enables* us to do things but it does not *force* us to. Its impact on society depends on the social circumstances in which it is made available.

History is littered with examples of technologies that could have had an effect on society but which never became widespread. 3D films and stereophonic television are both possible technologies that have not, for different reasons, become widely available. Conversely, manufacturers were taken by surprise at the demand for domestic video recorders. It is not only demand that effects the spread of technology. Technology is not free to develop without restriction. The path its development takes is shaped by the actions of powerful groups and interests in society.

In their account of the development of Euston Films, a subsidiary of the British Thames Television Company, Alvarado and Stewart (1985) explain why the company opted for the now somewhat old-fashioned technology of film rather than video. The decision was, they say, dictated by commercial rather than technological considerations. Film unions were prepared to operate more flexible working agreements than television unions.

Filmed productions could also be marketed overseas more easily. It is simpler to dub foreign language sound-tracks on to film than video. Furthermore there are three different television systems in the world (NTSC, PAL, and SECAM). Each is incompatible with the other two, so that programmes made on one system have to be transferred electronically before they can be broadcast. This makes film a much more 'marketable' commodity than video in the important international market for programmes.

Many of the new technologies of communication were originally developed for military purposes. Commercial manufacturers will often take out patents on ideas to prevent them being developed by competitors although they have no intention of using them.

By questioning technological determinism in accounts of social change, sociologists are not saying that technology has no social importance. What they are saying is that sociology should seek to describe and analyse the ways in which technological change interacts with the social, political, and economic contexts in which it occurs.

In the light of this cautionary advice we will examine some ideas on the impact of new media technologies.

Information technology

When people speak, as they do, of *the* new technology, they are referring to a particular branch of technological development within the field of electronics. The key to success in this area has been the ability to miniaturize large and complicated electronic circuits and components by etching them on to tiny wafers of silicon. Miniaturization has made possible the computer; a machine that can rapidly process and store large amounts of information (words, pictures, numbers) by following a set of instructions (program).

Associated with this has been the development of better methods of communicating this information across large distances using satellites and specially designed cables. These permit vast amounts of information to be passed at great speed between two points. The main stimulus for these developments has been the administrative and communication needs of the state (particularly the military sector), and multinational corporations. These improved techniques of handling and communicating information are known collectively as *information technology*.

These new technologies have made possible a transformation of the techniques of mass and individual communication. In the newspaper industry, for example, it could be possible for journalists to type their stories directly into a machine that then composes the type from which the paper is then printed. Such changes have been strongly resisted in Britain by print workers on national daily newspapers, many of whom would be made redundant if the new technology were to be implemented. Further, the printed word could be distributed in electronic form to households to appear and be read on TV screens; the so-called *electronic newspaper*.

In accordance with our earlier warnings of technological determinism, it must be pointed out that whether such possible changes become a reality depends on a variety of wider social, political, and commercial factors. We will look at some of these in relation to the new technologies of broadcasting.

New technology and broadcasting

It is clear from this example that new technology may be used to bring about serious changes in existing media services. This is particularly true of broadcasting.

At present Britain has four television channels (two operated by the BBC and two by the IBA). Signals are transmitted by a network of hundreds of local transmitters and received by an aerial attached directly to the television set. Four national radio channels are broadcast by the BBC in a similar manner. Since 1973 sixty local radio stations have been licensed, some operated by commercial organizations and some by the BBC.

Four television channels is about the maximum technically possible without impairing picture quality. However, cable television and direct broadcasting by satellite (DBS) could greatly extend the number of channels that could be received.

A cable system is a wired network connecting broadcasters to audiences. The media consumer has the option of being connected to this network in the same way as they may be connected to mains gas, telephone, electricity, or water services. Like the latter services, there will be those who cannot afford connection, or who live in areas too remote to be served. In the case of the cable system proposed for Britain at least 50 per cent of the population are expected to fall into this category.

The new cable system, unlike the existing telephone network, will be able to carry at least thirty channels of television – hence the name *broadband cable* – and so, it is argued, greatly enhance viewer choice. The British government published the Hunt Report (1982) which recommended the rapid construction of such a cable network by private enterprise. The Report was the work of a committee made up mainly of representatives of organizations involved in media technology. It did not conduct detailed market research or consult political parties, trades unions, or consumer organizations.

Satellites are similar to ground transmitting stations but

because of their height – 23,000 miles above the Earth's surface – are able to transmit signals across great distances to large numbers of viewers. One such satellite can broadcast to Britain and much of Europe. Communications satellites are placed in a precise orbit that keeps them in a fixed position above the ground. Thus they rotate at exactly the same speed as the Earth and television signals beamed up to them are bounced back to another point on the Earth surface.

Communications satellites have been used since the early 1960s to transmit television pictures between continents. Incoming satellite signals from America, for example, are picked up by a large receiving dish in Britain and then broadcast via the network of ground transmitters to the national television audience. A dramatic illustration of this was the 'Live Aid' charity pop concert (July 1985) which, using satellite communication, was available 'live' to 95 per cent of the world's television sets.

DBS is a recent refinement of this technique of satellite communication. A new generation of satellites producing a signal that is ten times stronger will be able to relay television programmes directly to the viewer. Signals would be received by a small (90 cm) receiving dish replacing the conventional aerial. The rights to operate two DBS channels have been granted to both the BBC and the IBA. As with cable, much of the pressure for DBS has come from the mainly American multinational corporations who expect large profits from these new communications satellites.

It is also possible for companies operating cables systems to receive satellite transmissions and then distribute them through their cable networks. In the USA there are forty satellite-delivered channels available to cable operators. In Europe twenty channels are expected to be available by 1986 (Burkitt 1985).

Interactive cable services

Broadband cables and DBS have the potential to expand

enormously the range of channels available to viewers. However, their uses go beyond this. They are very flexible communications highways, as they are not restricted to carrying 'one-way' traffic or mass media products. Communications satellites also carry international telephone calls – thousands of calls in both directions can be relayed simultaneously by existing satellites. Other kinds of information can also be relayed in *digital* form (the 'language' of computers) via satellite.

Broadband cables will be able to carry, in addition to thirty television channels, a variety of other 'cable services'. These depart from our original definition of the mass media (p. 15) as a one-way communication flow, for they are *interactive*. Like the telephone, messages will be able to be passed in both directions. Customers will be able to select and buy goods and services, receive and send information, or be consulted for their opinion on issues by these capacious and accommodating cables. Hence the popular scenario of the 'information society' (Bell 1976) where working, shopping, banking, and access to the world's knowledge will all become available from within the home.

It is claimed, using the logic of technological determinism, that broadband cable and DBS will have two connected effects. First, that they will improve mass media output by extending consumer choice and second, that they will bring economic revival to those countries that install them by stimulating demand for hardware (electronic equipment) and software (programme-making and information and data services) industries. For the future, in the view of Bell and many politicians, the biggest expansion of jobs and the best hopes for future prosperity lie with these 'information industries'. Critics are sceptical about the benefits of these new technologies, and they also fear their effects on the survival of existing media organizations.

British television has been regarded by many as a success in terms of the quality of programmes produced and the sales of such software abroad. Collins (1983b) suggests several reasons for this. The limited number of channels meant that large audiences and thus revenues could be assured. Quotas on the import of foreign (mostly American) programmes have kept them to 20 per cent of those broadcast. This has meant there was a stable demand for home-produced material. The growth in the number of channels since BBC television was established in 1946 has been gradual (ITV 1955, BBC2 1964, Channel 4 1982). This allowed production capacity to keep up with distribution capacity.

Collins argues that the explosive growth in the number of channels available as a result of cable and DBS will create a distribution system that outgrows the capacity of production. The large audiences that currently watch the four British channels will then be spread thinly among the dozens available. Money available for programme production will be reduced and so consequently will programme quality – more repeat programmes, programmes made to previously successful 'formulae', and fewer unusual, expensive, or contentious programmes.

Americanization of the media

America has the largest television audiences and the US television companies can cover their production costs in this enormous home market. They are able to offer expensively produced programmes to the broadcasting systems of other countries at cheap rates:

> 'An hour of original material can range from around £20,000 for a current affairs programme to £200,000 for drama (or even more in the case of prestige projects). Bought in from the USA, where the production costs have already been largely if not wholly covered on the domestic market, these can be obtained by broadcasters for as little as £2,000 an hour.'

> (HMSO 1983)

Far from stimulating British television production, an increase in the number of channels and the exposure of the British industry to international market forces will debase programme quality and destroy the home industry. Much the same has already happened, says Collins, to the British film industry.

Moreover the demand for interactive cable services is far from proven. So far, such services have not grown nearly as fast as expected. Nor is the need for a new cable network proven. With improvements, the existing British Telecom system could provide virtually all the services proposed.

Of course, if Collins is correct in arguing that cable and DBS will destroy even Britain's successful and well-established software industries, then the effects of the new communication technologies on other countries and especially on the poorest may be yet more dramatic.

Media organizations

So far, we have been concerned mainly with the world that surrounds the media organization — with the pressures and influences that come from outside.

What's missing from this outsider's view is any discussion of the media organizations themselves and the people who work within them. Chibnall (1977) argues that Marxist sociologists have tended to ignore this dimension. If, as Marxists claim, the media express a dominant ideology, how is this reproduced in the offices, board rooms, studios, news rooms, and editing suites of the mass media?

Certainly media workers do not, on the whole, see themselves as willing servants of the ruling classes conspiring to mislead and mystify the public. Neither do they see themselves as being forced unwillingly to follow orders from above. Many take pride in their professional standards and independence, their freedom to follow creative initiatives, their sensitivity and responsibility to their audiences. Journalists jealously guard against direct state intervention — many British television news workers were prepared to take strike action to protest when, in August 1985, the government brought pressure on the BBC to ban a documentary programme 'Real Lives' which included an interview with a known IRA supporter.

In the study of the mass media a great deal more effort has been put in to researching news than any other area of media output. Hence many of the references in this chapter are to the news media.

News gatekeepers

News rooms, like many other industrial workplaces, are complex organizations made up of a hierarchy of specialist staff. There are those who have a responsibility for particular contributions, for instance crime, sports, politics, industrial and fashion stories. Others, such as editors and sub-editors, are responsible for selecting and putting together the finished product. The word 'gatekeeper' describes the role of those who make important decisions about which items are to be put into the paper or broadcast.

The model, first applied by White (1950), divides newsworkers into two groups: 'newsgatherers', the journalists and reporters who go out and get the stories, and 'news processors', who use their judgement to 'filter' this information. In this model, understanding 'what makes the gatekeeper tick', is the key to understanding how news gets produced. It spawned a number of studies of the factors which influence the decisions made by gatekeepers – their personal whims, the norms, rules, and conventions of the office, the pressure of time, the need to observe the law, and the need to make a profit.

The concept of the gatekeeper is now regarded as an oversimplification by many media sociologists. To begin with, the modern news organization probably has not one but many gatekeepers filtering the news in succession. Ex-broadcaster Stuart Hood suggests:

'[they] include the editor who decides on the day's

coverage, or the organiser who briefs the camera crews and reporters and allocates assignments, the film editor who selects the film to be included in the bulletin, the copytaster who chooses the stories from the tape to accompany the film, the sub-editor who writes the story and the duty editor who supervises the compilation of the bulletin, fixes the running order of the stories and gives it its final shape.'

(Hood 1972)

Because all these media workers tend to be drawn from the same sort of middle-class background, Hood argues that their view of events and of what is newsworthy is affected – they project an image of the world untroubled by major divisions of interest.

A more vital criticism of the gatekeeper model of news organizations is that it oversimplifies the role of the journalist. It is as though the reporter goes out 'picking up stories as if they were fallen apples' (Chibnall 1977). The reality, Chibnall argues, is very different. The journalist does not harvest a crop of stories thus turning them into news. Few news items are directly observed by the journalist. Most are derived from secondary sources – news agencies, official spokespeople – and are then 're-packaged' into a product, the news story. By concentrating on the gatekeepers we overlook the influences and pressures on journalists in selecting and processing events into news items – we overlook the fact that journalists don't just report but *create* the news.

News values

Whatever the limitations of the gatekeeper approach it did serve to direct the attention of media sociologists towards what goes on in the news room. How do journalists decide what makes an event 'newsworthy'? What are the routines by which events occurring in the 'real world' get transformed into news stories by newsworkers? The concept of news values has provided one of the most useful ways of approaching these questions.

93

Activity

For most of us, news is about other people and we accept what is reported because we have no other source of information. If you ever become the *subject* of a news report you may find your reactions are quite different.

Try to attend a newsworthy event (e.g. a meeting or demonstration) and compare your impressions with those of the news media. It will help if you take notes, photographs, and, if possible, film or video equipment and first construct your own report. This works best as a group activity.

Journalists are probably the worst people to ask about news values. They are usually unable to come up with a clear-cut answer as to what makes a story newsworthy. Journalists will often talk of their 'nose for news' – a kind of professional 'sixth sense' actually acquired through long experience. For the newsworker these unwritten rules of journalism are just professional common-sense. Along with many other skilled jobs, this common-sense acquires a certain mystique. It is built up gradually as the job is learnt. The novice journalist will spend many hours covering routine events, writing 'for the waste paper basket', under the supervision and guidance of editors and sub-editors, in the slow process of learning the 'craft of journalism'. Chibnall (1977) argues that the more important role of the editor and sub-editor is this socialization of new journalists into the news values of the organization, rather than that of gatekeeper.

The sociological understanding of news values has, therefore, come from observing journalists at work and analysing news rather than asking journalists direct questions. As Weber (1964) observed, bureaucracies tend to arrange their activities into standard procedures which deal with the work of the office in routine ways, although such routines may remain 'secrets of the office' concealed from outsiders. These unwritten rules do nevertheless exist.

Every bureaucracy has its own techniques for transforming the unpredictability of the real world into a set of routine processes. Schools turn education into subjects, timetables, and syllabuses. Hospitals turn sickness into diagnostic and treatment routines. News bureaucracies, however, face a uniquely difficult problem. The raw material of news is inherently unpredictable. News values serve to organize and give structure to the chaos of real world events, providing the newsworker with essential guidelines to the selection, construction, and presentation of the world in the news.

Bureaucratic routines

Certain news values seem to arise from the day-to-day business of the office. To be newsworthy, events must be compatible with institutional routines. One such routine is the obvious but important fact that most news rooms operate on a daily, twenty-four-hour cycle of production. Stories that develop gradually over a period of weeks, months, or years are less newsworthy than those which show a daily change. This has two consequences. Major but gradual social changes, for instance the growth in feminist consciousness, are less likely to be reported. If they are, it will be in terms of immediate events – an example is the coverage given to a small group of women who as a symbolic protest against their sexually defined roles publicly 'burned their bras'. This 'event orientation' (Galtung and Ruge 1981) has the effect of obscuring the background circumstances which led up to the event. Why should women suddenly burn their bras? Why should blacks in Britain or America suddenly turn on the police? Why should car workers suddenly go on strike? It has the effect of making the world seem a strange and irrational place.

News editors, like managers of any other bureaucracy, have to make decisions about the allocation of their resources – particularly staff resources. Decisions will have to be made about where journalists should be despatched in order to be in the best position to report stories. This involves the editor in the business of predicting what news is going to happen. This work is made considerably easier by fact that certain institutions are regular sources of news – law courts, sports events, parliamentary debates, press conferences. These institutional sources of news are much favoured by news-workers because they offer a reliable supply of stories. This dependence on official sources as a solution to the bureaucratic problems of the news media is one of the ways in which the views of the powerful acquire a privileged status in the media (see 'primary' and 'secondary' definers, p. 101).

The real world is not always so obliging in supplying stories to journalists in the field. Bureaucratic decisions about the allocation of staff may force the news room to construct a story where none exists. Hence the not unusual situation of a TV journalist, expensively set up outside an important meeting, reporting, in a live insert to the news broadcast, that . . . nothing has happened! Management decisions concerning the placement of staff can thus influence which stories are included.

Another feature of the bureaucratic form that modern organizations take, according to Weber, is that their staff is made up of specialists who have specific areas of responsibility and competence. In the case of news organizations there are reporters who deal with different news topics – sports, crime, economic and industrial, fashion, political, educational, and foreign correspondents. These specialist roles tie up with separate sections of the newspaper or broadcast. Whether a news item gets included will depend, in part, on whether it fits one of these preconceived news categories which daily have to be filled. Stories which might otherwise have a relatively low priority will be included to maintain the conventional proportions of different categories.

Activity

1 Take copies of the same daily paper for a week or so and

compare the space given over to 'home' and 'foreign' news. Over a period of time the proportions of the paper taken up by each category should remain quite stable.

2 The same can be done for broadcast news by timing the length of items in these categories.

Conventions of the medium also affect the newsworthiness of stories. Sub-editors may include a story, or give it a higher priority, if it is accompanied by a vivid photograph or dramatic piece of newsfilm to heighten the impact or give the right balance of words and pictures. A convention of television news broadcasts is to end on a 'lighter note' – a humorous or human interest story. Such 'aesthetic considerations' may give a news item a position in the paper or broadcast that it might otherwise not merit.

It is not only newsworkers who have to operate within bureaucratic constraints. In the case of adult drama on British Independent Television, the length and placement of programmes is fixed at one hour scheduled between 9.00 and 10.00 p.m. Three factors produce this result: first, the Independent Broadcasting Authority's Family Viewing Policy requires programmes 'unsuitable for children' to be broadcast after 9.00 p.m.; second, 'News at Ten' is always at the same time; and third, the need to attract a large audience rules out later scheduling of broadcasts. As a result, a convention of one-hour formats for programmes such as 'Minder', 'The Sweeney', and 'Reilly, Ace of Spies', has emerged (Alvarado and Stewart 1985).

'Satisfying customers'

In their search for audience appeal, reporters aim for dramatic effect. As many a political protestor has discovered, it's not so much the *cause* as the *fact* of the demonstration that the media are interested in. Scenes of emotion and especially violence are given a primary position, while the protestors'

97

arguments and rationale are secondary. On 19 January, 1981 a fire at a party of mostly black people in New Cross, London, killed fifteen people and injured a further thirty. Public dissatisfaction with the way the police were investigating the case grew to a head with a march through central London. Patricia Holland (1981), in an analysis of the press coverage of these events, showed how they were presented in the dramatic terms of a 'race riot'. Only cursory reference was made to the cause of the marchers. This can also be seen as an example of racial stereotypes in the media (see pp. 48–51).

News items are also presented in personal terms. Political and industrial conflicts are reduced to conflicts between personalities – Reagan vs Carter, Scargill vs McGregor. It is assumed that:

> ' "ordinary people" can only grasp the meaning of abstractions when they are presented in vivid personalised terms which allow for identification. Thus inflation becomes intelligible by examining its effect on the housekeeping of a Greater London housewife, while violence can be understood through an interview with a mugger's victim.'
>
> (Chibnall 1977)

The classic vehicle for the themes of drama and personality is another news value: the media's concern with the sexual and immoral. Stories of sexual 'goings on' attract and titillate audiences, inflame and confirm prejudices, and reassure by finally condemning.

We have noted already (see p. 38) that there is a hierarchy of access to the media. The views of the powerful receive more credibility in the media than those of other groups. This is perhaps the origin of another news value, that stories concerning élite persons, groups, and nations are more newsworthy. Stories concerning royal families, presidents, stars and famous personalities, the rich and powerful nations of the west, and affluent sections of the community are more likely to be reported than those concerning ordinary people.

This reflects in part the allocation of journalistic resources including those of the big five international news agencies: Associated Press, United Press International, Agence France-Presse (see p. 80), Reuters, and the Soviet Union's Tass. These provide news stories to 90 per cent of the world's television and radio stations but concentrate their resources in the west. For example, 62 per cent of news agency staff are located in Europe and the USA, and only 4 per cent in Africa. Hence journalists are generally less well-informed and up to date on Third World events. This will be reflected in the stories they write.

The social construction of news

News values provide some answers to the question of how newsworkers pick out some events in the real world as newsworthy. Events which possess some of these qualities are likely to be selected as newsworthy. Furthermore the most newsworthy events are those which score high on *all* these news values. Such events will be guaranteed a high degree of news exposure and a high priority in news bulletins – front-page treatment or the first item in the running order of a news broadcast.

Activity

You might like to test the accuracy of this assertion by considering a news item that has received a great deal of media attention. A good indicator of such stories in broadcast news is whether the story is considered sufficiently important to spill over the normal limits of programming and so interrupt scheduled broadcasts – the 'newsflash'. Take a story that has achieved such prominence and check whether it possesses all the news values we have discussed so far.

These news values will also influence the way in which events are presented by the news media. Consequently journalists will seek to highlight the topical, dramatic, titillating, and personality aspects, etc., of any news story.

Media organizations, of course, differ in the ways in which they present the same story. Each has its own 'house style' which reflects its political stance and the combination of news values which has become its familiar trademark. But whatever their relative emphasis, the more important point is that all news organizations share these values.

All the news that's fit to print

The news media do not provide a 'mirror on the world'. They are actively involved in creating news and constructing a version of what is happening in the real world. The events they report are not left to speak for themselves. As Hall *et al.* (1978) argues, they seek to make these events meaningful and comprehensible to their audience.

They do this by two connected processes. First events are identified: they are named, defined, and related to other events – another 'mugging', 'terrorist attack', or case of 'child abuse'. This labels the event and simultaneously rules out alternative ways of seeing it. 'Mindless industrial militants' cannot, therefore, be responding rationally to hardship and exploitation. In Holland's report (see p. 98) the prior identification of black youth as 'violent' and 'muggers' made it impossible for them to be perceived by the media as the *victims* of a racial attack.

Once identified, the media then place the event in a familiar context: another example of the way in which 'selfish and greedy union militants are undermining the British economy', another example of the 'declining moral standards of the young'. Reported events are thus placed on a 'cultural map of meaning' (Hall *et al.* 1978), and although these maps may vary somewhat between different organs of the mass media they all share a *consensual image of society*. That is they share the view that we all see things in the same way, that there are no significant conflicts of interest that cannot be reconciled within the existing structure of society.

The familiar labels and contexts of the media provide the basis for a final important news value: events are more likely to be reported if they can be slotted in to an existing framework. In this way reality is 'bent' to fit the familiar consensus view of the world the media project. 'Instead of aiding his audience to come to terms with old realities in new ways, the journalist now tends to help his audience come to terms with new realities in old ways' (Chibnall 1977). In this sense, as Galtung and Ruge (1981) remark, 'news' is to some extent 'olds'.

According to Hall, the process of identifying reported news events and placing them in context both assumes and helps to construct this consensus. This is because of the relationship the media have towards the institutional sources of news stories. These are the powerful 'primary definers' of news. Their views provide raw material upon which editors and journalists (the secondary definers) can then work: 'The media thus tend, faithfully and impartially, to reproduce symbolically the existing structure of power in society's institutional order' (Hall *et al.* 1978).

This does not mean that dissenting voices are never heard in the mass media. Trades unions, for example, by dint of organized struggle, have won the right to express an alternative view although this has to be set within the terms established by the primary definers (see pp. 53–4).

The view that the mass media play a crucial role in sustaining the status quo in society by presenting a consensual view of the world has been criticized. Young (in Cohen and Young 1981) argues that it places too much responsibility on the mass media. This 'left functionalist' view of the media assumes that their function is simply to reflect the interests of the powerful. It overlooks the ways in which the media may sometimes present views which are dysfunctional to (against the interests of) the state and ruling class. The ideas of ordinary people, according to Young, are controlled not so much through the images present in the mass media as through the material world of inequality. The media may reflect and reinforce the consensus – they do not create it. Finally it overlooks the active role of the audience whose interests must be taken on board if they are to be persuaded to consume the media product. We will return to this issue in the final chapter.

Further reading

Part 1 of Curran and Seaton (1981) provides a readable account of the growth of the British press and the importance of commercial pressures, while part 2 gives the history of broadcasting. Aubrey (1981) tells the story of two journalists who found themselves up against the law for looking too closely into areas forbidden by the state. Murphy (1983), Sieghart (1982), and Curran and Seaton (1985) pursue some of the issues connected with the impact of new technologies on the media. Cohen and Young's book (1981) is a valuable, but not always easy collection of readings that examines how, and with what effect, the news media depict crime and deviance. At a more entertaining level, Michael Frayn's (1965) novel provides a wry slant on the business of journalism seen through the eyes of an insider.

4

Media research

The shortcomings of past studies of the media have convinced recent sociologists of the need to find better ways of approaching the topic. In their search for alternative methods they have drawn upon other disciplines. This chapter reports on some of the tools used by sociologists to examine the media.

Content analysis

Content analysis is similar, in many ways, to the more familiar social science survey. It is not surprising, therefore, that content analysis shares many of the social survey's weaknesses.

Further reading

See McNeill (1985) for a fuller account of survey techniques in sociology.

Essentially a content analysis is a counting exercise. It answers the question: 'how often does "x" occur in the media?' How often do women appear in positions of authority; how often are employers seen to be responsible for industrial disputes? The results that are produced are often in the form of a rate – so many deaths per hour in television police dramas – and they only begin to make sense when we have an opportunity to compare one rate with another – men against women, 'cop' stories against cartoons, comedies, or commercials. Content analysis is most successful when dealing with such broad generalizations. But, as with the survey, what is gained in breadth is often lost in the depth of the analysis possible.

The Glasgow University Media Group (GUMG)

Most content analysis has been of written forms of the media. The GUMG study (Glasgow University Media Group 1976) is one of a number of more recent studies of television made possible by the advent of the domestic video recorder. Although content analysis may seem a straightforward 'head counting' procedure, there are considerable difficulties in putting the technique into practice.

The choice of topic

Funded by a grant from the British Social Science Research Council, the GUMG set out to investigate the claim, close to the hearts of most broadcasters, that television news reporting was impartial and objective. This was a proposition which the GUMG felt had received little empirical investigation. What evidence was there for Gerbner's statement that mass communications 'are the cultural arm of the industrial order from which they spring'? (quoted in Glasgow University Media Group 1976) The world of work is a source of many conflicts. Thus the GUMG reasoned that a study of industrial news would provide a good test case for the claim that television reporting was impartial and unbiased.

Choice of sample

The group chose as a sample of programmes all British television news broadcasting for one year, looking in detail only at industrial and economic news stories. In the event this was reduced to six months as the group found the task of analysing such large quantities of data beyond their resources. Critics have claimed that this sample was unrepresentative because there was an unusually high level of disputes in certain industries at that time.

Categorizing stories

This is one of the most difficult areas of content analysis. Which are the relevant categories, can they be known in advance of the research, and how to deal with items that don't fit? The group made some preliminary studies based on the professional experience of some of their members. A draft of twenty-four categories was produced and modified after some initial testing.

A data sheet was produced on to which information was to be logged, recording the length, placement, and running order of news items, its category (e.g. 'crime', 'industrial', 'disasters', etc.), who presented it, what interviewers were involved, and what use was made of news film.

Several difficulties arose with the categorization and recording of data: the same story often appeared in different categories according to the 'news angle' adopted by the news room, and stories were often bundled together by broadcasters into a 'package'. Thus three separate industrial disputes would appear linked together in one news item.

The eight members of the research team did their own data collection, completing the log and storing video copies of industrial and economic stories for later analysis and checking.

105

Technical breakdowns and human error led to the loss of about 6 per cent of broadcasts. Random checks were made to ensure that all the group were categorizing in the same way. This did not answer the criticism that the group may have been tempted to categorize items to give the results they expected. Much of the information from the log was given a numerical code so that patterns could be discovered and analysed by computer.

A major difficulty for the project was the suspicion with which it was viewed by the broadcasting authorities. This developed into outright hostility on the publication of its findings. This attitude was a significant obstacle which prevented the group from carrying out the planned observation of news room activity.

When reporting the research the group drew upon official statistics of industrial disputes as a point of comparison. (See pp. 53–4 for an account of their findings.)

Evaluation

Adopting scientific techniques for the study of the media introduces an artificial note. Just as the formal questionnaire is a contrived form of social interaction, content analysis is an unnatural and artificial way of looking at the media. We do not normally scan large tracts of media output for particular categories of items. In seeking to isolate and categorize 'particles' of media output, content analysis is in danger of taking items out of context.

The strengths of content analysis are its ability to take an 'aerial' view of a familiar terrain, bringing to our notice patterns that were previously concealed, and the scientific rigour of its procedures. Its weakness lies in the fact that some aspects of the media lend themselves much more easily to counting than others. We should be wary also of assuming that the events which occur most frequently in the media are necessarily the most important. It deals best with the manifest or obvious aspects of what the media are saying to us, but is unable to deal with subtler shades of meaning.

The GUMG recognized the limitations of the method and turned to other forms of analysis (such as semiology) in the later stages of the project, particularly in their attempt to analyse the language and visual presentation of news programmes.

Although limited in its scope, content analysis remains a useful tool for media researchers. The results it produces often forms the starting-point for more detailed and delicate probings of the media's messages.

Semantic differential

Semantics is a branch of linguistics (the study of language) which is concerned with the meaning of words. The semantic differential is a method, borrowed from psychology, for measuring the meaning that media content has for audiences. Like content analysis, the findings it produces become useful only when compared between different audience sections or different media items.

The technique is quite simple. First a number of dimensions of meaning is established relevant to the item being studied. Each meaning dimension will be labelled with a descriptive word at each end. Words at opposite ends of a dimension of meaning will have opposite meanings. For example:

```
        1  2  3  4  5  6  7
warm    ........................................    cold
relaxed ........................................    tense
expert  ........................................    inexpert
```

When about a dozen of these dimensions have been established they are presented to a representative sample of the audience. The audience is shown the media item and asked to place their reaction in terms of each of the dimensions on a scale of one to seven. One or seven would indicate strong agreement with one or other of the meanings, shading off to a neutral judgement at the mid-point (4). When a sufficient number of these is collected an average response is calculated for each dimension.

Activity

You could use this method to assess the meanings of different advertisements, perhaps for the same product. Begin by holding an open-ended discussion of the advertisements with members of the audience. A tape-recording of this is then used to generate the various dimensions of meaning used in the second stage.

Similar techniques are used to establish the uses audiences make of the media. As a method it suffers from similar shortcomings to those of the uses and gratifications approach (see pp. 124–25).

Neither of the above methods has the 'fine tuning' necessary to reveal the deeper ideological messages of the mass media. For that, media researchers have developed a completely different set of analytical instruments.

Semiology

Semiology has been defined as: 'a science which studies the life of signs within society'. If, as suggested above, content analysis resembles the sociological survey in its broad-ranging quantitative approach, the method of semiology is equivalent to the detailed, participant-observation study in that it offers a way of analysing, in depth, the meanings that lie within a particular text. (A text is a general term used by semiologists to describe a media message, whether it is in the form of printed words, a radio or television programme, film, etc.).

In every-day conversation we may demand of others to 'say what you mean' or 'speak your mind'. Semiology starts from the assumption that such direct communication between human beings is impossible. Whenever we communicate we do so in codes. Morse code, sign languages used by people with impaired hearing, and the feelings and attitudes we show or 'give away' in our gestures, movements, and facial expressions (which psychologists refer to as non-verbal communication) are each examples of such codes. A code has two parts: the basic units of the code, and a set of rules which lay down how these units should be put together when used in communication. In the jargon of semiology these units are known as signs. For example, in that most important of codes, language, the basic units (the signs), are the words which make up its vocabulary. The rules, in this case, are the rules of grammar which say how words should be joined together to produce a verbal communication which makes sense to others.

A typical feature of codes is that the more familiar we are with them the more natural and obvious they seem. Like any other human skill, codes are 'easy when you know how'. Using a code becomes second nature to the skilled user just as an experienced motorist is largely unaware of the skills involved in driving. It is because the codes we use become so automatic that we forget that we are using them. This is fine if all we are concerned with is convenience, but, as the semiologist points out, if we wish to understand the codes we use, then the fact that we are unaware of them is an obstacle. Semiology sets out to produce techniques that will remind us of the vocabulary and grammar of the codes we use.

For sociologists, questioning what seems 'natural' or 'common-sense' is important because these are the murky waters in which ideology is so often concealed. Let us take the case of language. Most of the time the words that we use, the signs of the code of English, seem natural, neutral, and obvious. But if we look more closely we find that there are conventions such as the use of 'him' to describe men *and* women, that the word 'master' has different meanings from the word 'mistress', and that it is possible to list many negative words to describe women but few equivalent negative words for men.

Activity

Make a list of all the negative words that you can recall to describe women ('bitch', 'whore', 'scrubber', etc.). When you run out of words try to produce a list of equivalents for men. You will probably find that our language gives us more terms of abuse for women and also that words describing the equivalent behaviour in men frequently lose their negative overtones. Why do you think this is so? (See Spender 1980.)

Paradigms and syntagms

Clothing is another code. The way we dress involves a series of choices. Like language these choices can be analysed into two types: firstly, choices about what to wear, in that we select individual items from shops in the long term and from our wardrobe in the short term – our 'vocabulary' of clothes – and secondly, choices about how to combine these items together to produce our overall appearance on any day. Semiologists use the term *paradigm* to describe the range of items from which we can choose and *syntagm* to describe the way these are put together according to certain rules. Notice that the meaning of a group of signs is a product of both these choices. In the 1960s there was a fashion among young people for wearing items of second-hand military clothing (camouflage jackets, dress uniforms, etc.), but when combined with long hair and old gym shoes they produced a non- or anti-military style that was intentionally shocking.

Activity

List the components (paradigm) of a recent dress style such as punk. How are these combined into a syntagm – can you discover any rules for putting together individual items of clothing in the punk style?

110

We are probably not always conscious that in putting on clothes we are constructing a coded communication. Many people (particularly men) will protest that they just wear the first thing that comes to hand. It is the task of semiology to reveal the choices that are involved in any code and then to link these to the structure of society.

Semiology began as a method for studying language. Ferdinand de Saussure (1974) first coined the term but the recent development of this 'science of signs' has been as a method for analysing other forms – particularly film, advertising and publicity, photography, and television. One reason for its success and popularity as a means of studying mass media is that, unlike older traditions of literary analysis, it does not start from the assumption that popular culture is inferior. Another is that it is a flexible tool, one which can equally be applied to words, sounds, and pictures.

Realism

One obstacle people often encounter when thinking about film, television, and other popular culture in semiological terms is the idea of realism. Early westerns – cowboy films – often showed heroes in white hats and villains in black hats. We recognize now, without difficulty, that this was a code which provided a sort of visual shorthand for who were the 'goodies' and the 'baddies', and that, in real life, 'good' and 'evil' are not nearly so easily recognizable. The convention was so widely adopted that it became a cliché (an over-used stereotype).

By contrast, it is commonly argued, modern films and television programmes are much more realistic – they are 'true to life'. Semiologists argue, however, that 'realism' is simply another code that has its own paradigm (vocabulary of signs). For example the 'grainy' images that make up the opening credits of 'The Sweeney' or 'Minder' on television, the use of 'subjective' camera shots (where a jerky image is produced by the camera being carried by a moving camera operator) which give us the impression of being 'in on the action', the noisy sound-track of 'Hill Street Blues' with its background of conversations and crowded and confusing sets – all of these are codes that invite us to view the 'text' as more realistic.

Sign = signifier + signified

The basic unit of semiological analysis is the sign. This has two parts: the physical object that we perceive through our senses (the signifier), and the thing that object represents to us, its meaning (the signified). For example, the signifier could be the block of shaded dots that make up a newspaper photograph, or the word: 'Maggie'. Each can be signifiers of the same signified, the British Prime Minister.

Arbitrary and iconic signifiers

The photograph has a more direct relationship to the thing it stands for. Most of us have little difficulty in recognizing a person from a photographic image of their face. Signifiers that resemble the thing they represent (their signified) are known as *iconic*. Their meaning can be 'read' quite directly and requires less prior experience to understand.

However,, there is no such direct connection between the word 'Maggie' and the thing it represents. The word, whether written or spoken, does not look like or sound like its meaning – it does not resemble its signified. We only connect the two because we have learnt the code – language. Without such knowledge, 'Maggie' would just be a meaningless pattern of shapes or sounds. Such signifiers are known as *arbitrary*, because there is no necessary connection between what they are and what they represent.

The vocabularies of most languages are arbitrary. There are, of course, some words which, when pronounced, sound like the thing they represent. It is possible to detect a direct connection between words like 'plop', 'tinkle', 'gush' and their meanings. But in most cases we know the meaning of words only because we have learnt them.

The distinction between arbitrary and iconic signs is not, however, a hard and fast one. Consider the sign that shows the black silhouettes of two walking children on a white triangular background with a red border. It is partly iconic – the figures *are* childlike, but we are relying also on our familiarity with this simplified form of the human figure. Furthermore, its meaning as a road sign: 'warning children crossing' depends on our having learnt the language of road signs – the highway code.

All signs have an arbitrary element. We have to learn certain conventions even to decode a photograph, however iconic it may appear. It is, after all, unlikely to be life-size in scale, it is often just black and white, and it is always two-rather than three-dimensional.

To return to our first example, newsworkers will have a choice from a vocabulary (paradigm) of words to signify the British Prime Minister: 'Maggie', 'Margaret', 'Mrs Margaret Thatcher', 'Mrs Thatcher', 'Mrs T.', 'the Prime Minister', 'the Iron Lady' and so on. There will also be a choice to be made from a paradigm of photographic images taken to illustrate the story or from the news room's library of shots.

What the sign connotes

The choice of one sign rather than another is clearly an important decision. Each sign has a limited range of meanings and carries with it a particular slant or association. Semiologists refer to this as its *connotation*. The selection of the word 'Maggie' has a number of connotations. As a shortened form of 'Margaret' it suggest familiarity. It is a form that is widely used among the working class – in contrast, say, to 'Meg' with its rural, middle-class associations. The connotations of informality and ordinariness have made it a suitable form of address for opponents and supporters alike. The connotations of a sign are not, therefore, fixed. The term 'Iron Lady', originally meant to connote her inflexibility and dogmatism, has also been transformed by her protagonists to connote strength and steadfast resolution (particularly during the Falklands/Malvinas conflict).

Activity

1 Take another public figure often referred to in the mass media. List the alternative words used to signify this person and describe their different connotations.
2 Examine the paradigm of images used to signify 'Christmas' in, for example, greetings cards, gift wrapping, or product advertising. What different connotations of the event 'Christmas' are implied by these different signifiers? A comparison with old Christmas cards or those of another country would be an interesting extension to this activity.

'Open' and 'closed' texts

The meanings that are associated with particular signs can change and and may become the focus for an ideological struggle. But mass media forms such as newspapers attempt to avoid ambiguity by limiting the range of alternative meanings possible.

In reporting an event such as the dispute between the British coal-miners and the National Coal Board, the media on the whole offered accounts that favoured some interpretations (the right of the non-striking miner to work, a narrow definition of 'uneconomic' pits) over others.

Italian semiologist Umberto Eco (1981) argues that texts such as these, because they encourage strongly a particular interpretation or 'reading', are *closed texts* – our understanding of them is directed to follow a particular preferred route.

Symbolic 'road-blocks' deter us from diverting. Thus, although it is not *impossible* to select an alternative route, those who do so encounter more obstacles. Closed texts work by appealing to those things we have in common as members of a particular culture. They reassure and comfort us through what we already know – they both draw upon and help to reinforce our sense of belonging.

Other media forms, especially those concerned with notions of 'art' (novels, films, plays, and even many advertisements), are more open in the sense that they allow (or 'prefer' to use the semiologist's terms) a number of simultaneous interpretations. According to Eco, they thrive on an uncertainty or ambiguity of meaning and encourage the reader to produce a subjective response to the text. Writers such as Morley (1980) remind us that in all cases, whether the text is open or closed, audiences may adopt different interpretations of media products which reflect the particular social and economic position of the reader (see pp. 125–27).

Syntagms

Of course, our understanding of a particular text does not come simply from adding up the meanings of the individual signs. Take the sentence you have just read. Its meaning does not come only from the individual words but from the way they are *combined together* according to the rules of grammar (I hope!). Thus 'dogs chase cats' does not mean the same as 'cats chase dogs' even though the words are exactly the same. The combination of signs into wider patterns of meaning is known as a *syntagm*.

The same is true of images. The way a film director arranges a series of shots in a sequence (a process known as *montage*) produces a particular meaning. A close-up of an actor's face which 'dissolves' into another scene usually means that we are entering the character's thoughts, dreams, or memories. Through our familiarity with the 'grammar' of film we infer these interpretations almost automatically.

Images of smartness, affluence, status, modernity, tradition, wholesomeness, freshness, sexual appeal, youth, family life, are used frequently to connote particular meanings in adverts.

1 Cut a selection of advertisements from magazines and illustrate how the above meanings can be generated from the combination of images.
2 The above list is not, of course, complete. See whether you can discover some others.

Anchorage

Images, as signs, are more open than words to alternative meanings. Media workers will frequently attempt to 'fix' a particular interpretation by the use of words – captions, headlines, or narrators. Stuart Hall (in Cohen and Young 1981) shows how the captions to news photographs tell us how to read the image (What is going on? What feelings are being expressed?). They tie down the possible range of meanings to one preferred reading. This process is described by the French semiologist Roland Barthes (1973) as *anchoring* an image.

Activity

Demonstrating this can be an amusing exercise.

1 Cut out a number of news photographs, substituting alternative captions you have found or made up. You could also 'get your own back' on the advertisers by changing the meaning of adverts in the same way.
2 Different newspapers will often use the same photograph to illustrate their stories. Collect a number of papers from the same day and compare the different captions used.
3 Notice also the different ways in which papers frame the

same photograph, by trimming the image down in different ways they are able to select their 'preferred reading'. You may like to experiment with this too. Does the camera 'never lie'?

Semiological analysis addresses itself to three sorts of questions: What are the basic units of the text – the signs? How are these combined to produce meaning? How are these meanings related to the social structure of society?

If you attempted the last exercise you may have discovered that images that connote 'health' and 'fitness' are currently quite common in advertising. The semiologist might, for example, seek to relate the popularity of this image to a society in which the values of self-reliance, individuality, and competition are highly valued.

Judith Williamson (1978) has argued that in many advertisements people are identified with products so closely that the two become interchangeable. The objects are made to speak for people ('Say it with flowers') or people become identified with products ('The Pepsi Generation'). People are encouraged as a result to identify with others in terms of what they consume rather than what they produce. One consequence of this may be to encourage what Marxists refer to as 'false class consciousness' – a failure to recognize one's true position in a class society as determined by the relations of production. If the combined effect of advertising is that people can be made to believe that owning a car, a colour television, or a washing machine makes them middle class then it is not just selling products; it is also serving the ideological function of 'selling' capitalism.

Further reading

Most of the literature in this area is quite complex and technical – simple introductions to semiology are scarce. You might try the relevant chapters in Fiske (1982) or Fiske and Hartley (1978). Fiske, Hartley, O'Sullivan, and Saunders'

(1983) glossary of communication terms is a useful guide when studying this topic.

Audience research

Semiologists, anxious to uncover the complex coding of media messages, suggested that certain audience interpretations were more likely, certain readings of the text were 'preferred'. From the first phase of media research they took the view that the media played a prominent role in shaping ideas, while recognizing the criticism, raised by the later 'two-step flow' researchers, that audiences were capable of putting forward alternative readings. Even so, the question of how certain members of audiences are able to produce alternative interpretations of media texts remains unanswered. What evidence is there that the 'preferred reading', carefully unravelled by the semiologist, is indeed the view that audiences actually take?

Horror comics re-visited

Let us return briefly to where we began. Barker (1984a), in his study of horror comics, analyses a few of the most notorious comic strips in some detail. He condemns the anti-comics campaigners for coming to rushed and superficial judgements. He claims that careful study of these texts reveals an underlying theme. They were 'exercises in doubt'; they used the techniques of suspense to shock us into questioning what we take for granted. As such they encouraged in their readers a questioning attitude – a healthy scepticism.

But how do we know that those who read these comics actually saw this side of them? If they did, what evidence do we have that it had such effects? What proportion of the audience read other meanings into the comics? Were some affected in the ways the anti-comics campaigners feared?

Similar questions can be raised about Barker's analysis of

the notorious 'video nasty', *I Spit on Your Grave* (Barker 1984b). This video has attracted criticism both from feminists for its 'degrading' treatment of women and from more conservative moral campaigners. Barker claims that careful analysis reveals a tale that supports a woman's right to a career and independence. But can we be sure that this is how audiences actually interpret the text?

In the case of the horror comics, very little is known even about who bought and read them. Barker suggests they were mainly working-class young adults. Horror comics are not unusual in this respect. There is quite a lot of data available about the size or composition of mass media audiences, but it is mostly data collected by media producers to convince shareholders and advertisers of the popularity of their products. Such information is often unsuited to the research needs of media sociologists.

Overall size of media audiences

A major difficulty in obtaining estimates here is the variety of different methods used to measure media audiences. For example, the two main producers of British television programmes, the BBC and ITV, were, until recently, engaged in a battle over the size of their respective audiences which resulted from the different systems of measurement employed by each side. The BBC had a very large representative sample of viewers which it interviewed in sections each week, while ITV used a system of meters attached to the television sets of a sample of viewers. This registered when, and for how long, sets were switched on and which channels were selected.

A joint system for measuring British television audience sizes now exists, operated by BARB (British Audience Research Board). This uses three types of measures: a meter system, diaries of programmes seen by representative samples of viewers, and interviews with representative samples to gauge their appreciation of programmes.

Tunstall (1983) proposes that we distinguish between three

types of audience when measuring the hours spent with different media. Firstly, a *primary audience* which consists of those people for whom the medium is a main focus of their current activity (e.g. listening carefully to the news). Next, a *secondary audience* which divides its attention between the medium and other activities (e.g. listening to the radio while doing housework). Finally, a *tertiary audience* which is only vaguely aware of the medium (e.g. catching 'snippets' of a programme playing in another room or glancing at newspaper headlines on a train).

Using these definitions, he has produced the following table to indicate the average hours spent with different media (Tunstall 1983: 135).

Table 1 *British adults: estimated average hours spent per week with major media, 1982*

	primary activity (narrow definition)	primary and secondary activity (looser definition)	primary, secondary, and tertiary activity (including set 'switched on', 'looking at', newspaper, etc.)
television	18[1]	21[2]	35[2]
radio	2	23[3]	30
newspaper and magazines	5	6	10
total hours per week	25	50	75

Sources: Tunstall's estimates based on: 1) BBC 1980; 2) BARB 1982; 3) JICRAR 1982.

Activity

Consider the different methods of estimating audience size

mentioned above and list some reasons why they might produce different or inaccurate results.

=====

Age

The age structure of audiences varies considerably for different mass media forms. The following diagram illustrates the main patterns of media consumption by age.

5–15..............	TV (high)
16+	TV (low)
	radio, records, and cinema (high)
20s................	regular daily paper (high)
(on marriage)	TV (high)
	cinema (low)
40s................	radio, TV, newspapers (high)
60s................	newspapers (high, declining rapidly after 65)
	radio (declining, Radio 4 popular)
	TV (high, especially children's TV and ITV)

(data from Tunstall 1983)

Time of day and year

Media consumption varies considerably with time of day. Early morning is the peak time for radio and·newspapers, with significant numbers now watching 'breakfast' television. Audiences for each of these are lower during the rest of the morning but rise again at lunchtime. Radio audiences decline further over the afternoon while the television audience steadily increases from mid-afternoon onwards as children return from school. In the evening radio audiences decline further but for a small increase as people go to bed, while television rises steeply to a peak between nine and ten o'clock, dropping off sharply thereafter.

Newspaper audiences are smaller on Saturday, but Sunday has the highest newspaper sales of the week. Saturday afternoon is the peak daytime television audience, while the large Sunday radio audience is at 10–11 a.m.

Seasonal changes in audience size also occur. With the exception of cinema, audiences are smaller in the summer, the average daily time spent watching television being half an hour less. The Christmas holiday produces the largest audiences for television.

Activity

Suggest some reasons for the different patterns of media consumption by day, week, and year outlined above.

Class and gender

For newspapers and television the audience is roughly divided between men and women, although there are differences within the media: sport and politics are more popular with men, while women's features and entertainment news are more popular with women. The advent of Channel 4 television has given rise to more specialized audiences. Magazine readership is often much more divided in gender terms. Sex magazines and most professional and technical magazines are read mainly by men. Women's magazines, which focus on the 'feminine concerns' of the home, fashion, beauty, and the family, are read mostly, but not exclusively, by women. Women's magazines, hit badly by a loss of advertising revenue to commercial television, still have large circulations – altogether over six million copies were sold each week in 1982.

Class profiles for newspapers suggest that national daily newspapers are very different in the class composition of their readership (see the figure reproduced below from Tunstall 1983: 77).

The major use of these statistics is to enable advertisers to 'target' particular sections of the purchasing public.

Figure 2 National newspaper readers: social class and age, 1981

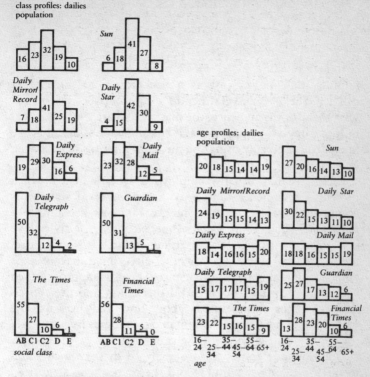

Source: Henry, H. (1982) Patterns and Trends of the National Newspaper Press. *Admap Publications* September: 501–16.

Further reading

The best instant source of British audience statistics is Tunstall (1983). Other sources are much more dispersed and require a good deal of interpretation.

Uses and gratifications

Bald statements of who reads what, and how often, provide, therefore, a very incomplete picture of audiences. 'Watching television', for example, might encompass a range of very different activities: filling in time, watching a selected programme, relaxing, as a pleasurable group experience, to impress someone, or just as a background to some other activity. The 'uses and gratifications' approach starts from the view that, for the audience, the mass media are a resource that is drawn upon to satisfy needs. It has an image of the audience in control, rationally using the media as a means of achieving its own ends.

Such research usually employs a questionnaire which presents an audience sample with a number of statements about their reasons for watching, reading, or listening to a particular media genre ('genre' means a type or style: love stories, soap operas, news programmes, etc.). It is, of course, important that these statements reflect the range of uses audiences might make of the media. The usual approach then is to tape-record an open-ended discussion and use this to devise a series of statements about how audiences use the media. Respondents are then invited to indicate how strongly they agree or disagree with the statement.

Questionnaire responses are analysed to see which statements are the most popular and these are then categorized into 'clusters'. Typical clusters are those reported by McQuail (McQuail, Blumler, and Brown 1972), who identified four main categories of use:

● Diversion and escape – from routines and problems.
● Personal relationships – the media provide company for the lonely, and topics for conversation.
● Personal identity – the media provide models and values that we can identify with or use as a point of comparison.
● Surveillance – the media satisfy a need to know what is going on in the world.

124

To ask audiences what uses they make of the media may seem an obvious direct approach, but it makes the rather large assumption that the audience is in control, that people know what they get out of the media, and that there are no hidden messages. It implies that we as audience members are completely free to make what we will of the media product – that there are no interpretations built in to media texts so they can mean what we want them to mean.

It also has tended to focus on the needs audiences have in common, rather than the different uses to which the media may be put by different social groups. Thus the needs that are identified are often in the form of bland psychological generalizations.

A *structural view* of audience response

Morley's (Morley 1980; Morley and Brunsdon 1978) study of the audience for the British news magazine programme 'Nationwide' is an attempt to combine the view that media texts do carry certain clear messages with the argument that audiences have some ability to make of the message what they will.

The research began with a semiological analysis of the style of the 'Nationwide' programme which included a detailed examination of particular programmes. In its style and content, 'Nationwide' presented a particular view of the world that emphasized the unity of the 'nation'. This was its preferred reading.

The semiological analysis was followed up by field research by interview in which Morley tried to establish whether audiences did in fact read the programme in this way. Do they use the same words in the same ways when talking about a news item? How far do they identify with the presenters and their summing up at the end of items? How far do they accept the general framework in which issues are presented? Do they accept the agenda set by the programme or were important issues left out? Finally, how are the answers to these questions related to nature of the news item and the age, sex, race, class, group, and cultural membership of the audience?

A recording of 'Nationwide' was shown to various groups of people. This was followed up by an open-ended group discussion which was tape-recorded. Morley sought to allow the group to define the terms of this discussion as far as possible, at first just listening and only later asking questions to clarify the positions they put forward.

In selecting the different groups Morley had in mind a theory put forward by Frank Parkin (Parkin 1973) concerning the effects of a dominant ideology on different segments of the population. This ideology holds a commanding position over all the major institutions of society: family, work, education, religion, and the media. Resistance to this dominant ideology is possible, but only where people are able to form cohesive groups – subcultures of opposition. Thus, Morley tried to find groups which represented a number of different subcultures to make up his audience sample.

Morley detected four main types of reaction to the programme. The first was shown in the responses of a group of working-class apprentices who, although critical of the formal middle-class tone of presentation, appeared to accept the agendas set by the programme. They saw the preferred reading as 'common-sense'. They were joined in this response by middle-class groups (bank managers, higher education students) who, while objecting to the tone of presentation ('undemanding entertainment/teatime stuff'), accepted the general framework of the programme.

A second type was illustrated by a group of full-time trades union officials whose response was described by Morley as 'negotiated'. While accepting in general the agendas set by the programme they objected to its representation of particular trades union issues.

A third group, of shop stewards (elected representatives rather than paid officials of the union), was critical, not only of specific issues – 'There's no discussion of investment, growth, production, creation of employment' – but also of the

126

entire consensus framework of the programme. 'they want the viewer, the average viewer, to all think . . . "we" . . .'; 'sort of soothing, jolly approach . . . as if you can take a nasty problem and just wrap it up . . . you know – "we're all in the same boat together"'. This was Morley's 'oppositional' response.

Finally a group of black students in further education appeared so distant from the terms of reference of the programme that they were not prepared even to oppose it. Theirs was a 'critique of silence' because the programme was irrelevant to their lives, intended for 'older', 'middle-class' people: 'I don't watch it, it's not interesting'; 'As soon as I see that man ['Nationwide' presenter] I just turn it over.'

Morley's two-stage research into the 'Nationwide' programme suggests a fruitful approach for media sociology. It offers a way of understanding how members of different groups respond to the dominant ideological messages of the media.

Further reading

Hartley, Goulden, and O'Sullivan (1985) contains a lot of useful information on the mass media which covers many of the areas of discussion raised in this book. Block three, units one and two are particularly relevant to the study of the audience, but the whole series is recommended, though not always easy, reading.

References

Adams, C. and Laurikietis, R. (1976) *The Gender Trap: Book 3 Messages and Images*. London: Virago.

Adorno, T.W., Frenkl-Brunswick, E., Levinson, D.J., and Sanford, R.N. (1950) *The Authoritarian Personality*. New York: Harper & Row.

Alvarado, M. and Stewart, J. (1985) *Made for Television: Euston Films Limited*. London: British Film Institute.

Aubrey, C. (1981) *Who's Watching You?* Harmondsworth: Penguin.

Barker, M. (1983) How Nasty Are the Nasties? *New Society* 10 November.

—— (1984a) *A Haunt of Fears*. London: Pluto Press.

—— (ed.) (1984b) *The Video Nasties: Freedom and Censorship in the Media*. London: Methuen.

Barnouw, E. (1978) *The Sponsor: Notes on a Modern Potentate*. New York: Oxford University Press.

Barthes, R. (1973) *Mythologies*. St Albans: Paladin.

Becker, H. (1963) *Outsiders: Studies in the Sociology of Deviance*. New York: Free Press.

—— (1967) Whose Side Are We On? *Social Problems* 14: 239–47.

Bell, D. (1976) *The Coming of the Post Industrial Society.* Harmondsworth: Peregrine.

Belson, W. (1967) *The Impact of Television.* London: Crosby Lockwood.

—— (1975) *Juvenile Theft: The Causal Factors.* London: Harper & Row.

—— (1978) *Television Violence and the Adolescent Boy.* Farnborough: Saxon House.

Blumler, J. (1979) An Overview of Recent Research into the Impact of Broadcasting in Democratic Politics. In M. Clark (ed.) *Politics and the Media.* Oxford: Pergamon.

Blumler, J. and McQuail, D. (1968) *Television in Politics: Its Uses and Influences.* London: Faber.

Bunce, R. (1976) *Television in the Corporate Interest.* New York: Praeger Publishers.

Burkitt, A. (1985) A Hitchhiker's Guide to Satellite Speak. *Broadcast* 5 July.

Burnham, J. (1960) *The Managerial Revolution.* Bloomington, Ind.: Indiana University Press.

Chibnall, S. (1977) *Law-and-Order News: An Analysis of Crime Reporting in the British Press.* London: Tavistock.

Cirino, R. (1973) Bias Through Selection and Omission: Automobile Safety, Smoking. In S. Cohen and J. Young (eds) *The Manufacture of News: Social Problems, Deviance and the Mass Media.* London: Constable.

Cohen, P. (1972) Subcultural Conflict and Working Class Community. Working Papers in Cultural Studies, 2, spring, Centre for Contemporary Cultural Studies, University of Birmingham.

Cohen, P. and Robins, D. (1978) *Knuckle Sandwich: Growing up in the Working Class City.* Harmondsworth: Penguin.

Cohen, S. (1972) *Folk Devils and Moral Panics: The Creation of the Mods and Rockers.* London: MacGibbon & Kee.

Cohen, S. and Young, J. (eds) (1981) *The Manufacture of News: Deviance, Social Problems and the Mass Media.* London: Constable (first edition 1973).

Collins, R. (1983a) 'Editorial'. *Media, Culture and Society* 5 (3/4 July–October).

—— (1983b) Broadband Black Death Cuts Queues. The Information Society and the UK. *Media, Culture and Society* 5 (3/4 July–October).

Curran, J. (1977) Capitalism and the Control of the Press 1800–1975. In J. Curran, M. Gurevitch, and J. Woollacott (eds) *Mass Communication and Society*. London: Edward Arnold.

Curran, J. (1982) Communications, Power and the Social Order. In M. Gurevitch, T. Bennett, J. Curran, and J. Woollacott (eds) *Culture, Society and the Media*. London: Methuen.

Curran, J. and Seaton, J. (1981/1985) *Power without Responsibility: The Press and Broadcasting in Britain*. London: Fontana (second edition 1985).

Curran, J., Gurevitch, M., and Woollacott, J. (eds) (1977) *Mass Communication and Society*. London: Edward Arnold.

Dyer, R. (1977) Stereotyping. In R. Dyer (ed.) *Gays and Film*. London: British Film Institute.

Eco, U. (1981) *The role of the Reader*. London: Hutchinson.

Eysenck, H. and Nias, D. (1980) *Sex, Violence and the Media*. London: Granada.

Ferguson, M. (1983) *Forever Feminine: Women's Magazines and the Cult of Femininity*. London: Heinemann.

Fiske, J. (1982) *Introduction to Communication Studies*. London: Methuen.

Fiske, J. and Hartley, J. (1978) *Reading Television*. London: Methuen.

Fiske, J., Hartley, J., O'Sullivan, D., and Saunders, D. (1983) *Key Concepts in Communication*. London: Methuen.

Frayn, M. (1965) *The Tin Men*. London: Collins.

Galtung, J. and Ruge, M. (1981) Structuring and Selecting News. In S. Cohen and J. Young (eds) *The Manufacture of News: Deviance, Social Problems and the Mass Media*. London: Constable.

Gerbner, G. (1972) Mass Media and Human Communication Theory. In D. McQuail (ed.) *Sociology of Mass Communications*. Harmondsworth: Penguin.

Gerbner, G., Gross, L., Signorelli, N., Morgan, M., and Jackson-Beeck. M. (1979) The Demonstration of Power: Violence Profile no. 10. *Journal of Communication* 29: 177–96.

Glasgow University Media Group (1976) *Bad News*. London: Routledge & Kegan Paul.

—— (1982) *Really Bad News*. London: Writers' & Readers' Cooperative.

Goffman, E. (1979) *Gender Advertisements*. London: Macmillan.

Golding, P. and Middleton, S. (1982) *Images of Welfare*, Oxford:

Martin Robertson.

Greenfield, P. (1984) *Mind and Media: The Effects of Television, Video Games and Computers*. London: Fontana.

Gurevitch, M., Bennett, T., Curran, J., and Woollacott, J. (eds) (1982) *Culture, Society and the Media*. London: Methuen.

Hall, S. (1981) The Determinations of News Photographs. In S. Cohen and J. Young (eds) *The Manufacture of News: Deviance, Social Problems and the Mass Media*. London: Constable.

Hall, S. (1982) The Rediscovery of 'Ideology': Return of the Repressed in Media Studies. In M. Gurevitch, T. Bennett, J. Curran, and J. Woollacott (eds) *Culture, Society and the Media*. London: Methuen.

Hall, S., Crichter, C., Jefferson, T., Clarke, J., and Roberts, B. (1978) *Policing the Crisis: Mugging, the State and Law and Order*. London: Macmillan.

Halloran, J. (ed.) (1970) *The Effects of Television*. London: Panther.

Halloran, J., Elliot, P., and Murdock, G. (1968) *Demonstrations and Communications: A Case Study*. Harmondsworth: Penguin.

Harris, R. (1983) *Gotcha! The Media, the Government and the Falklands Crisis*. London: Faber.

Hartley, J., Goulden, H., and O'Sullivan, T. (1985) *Making Sense of the Media*. London: Comedia.

Hartmann, P. and Husband, C. (1974) *Racism and the Mass Media*. London: Davis-Poynter.

—— (1981) The Mass Media and Racial Conflict. In S. Cohen and J. Young (eds) *The Manufacture of News: Deviance, Social Problems and the Mass Media*. London: Constable.

HMSO (1983) *The Development of Cable Systems and Services*. London: Cmnd 8866.

Hobson, D. (1980) Housewives and the Mass Media. In S. Hall, D. Hobson, A. Lowe, and P. Willis (eds) *Culture, Media, Language: Working Papers in Cultural Studies, 1972–79*. London: Hutchinson.

Holland, P. (1981) The New Cross Fire and the Popular Press. *Multiracial Education* (3).

Hood, S. (1972) The Politics of Television. In D. McQuail (ed.) *Sociology of Mass Communications*. Harmondsworth: Penguin.

Hunt Committee (1982) *Report on Cable Expansion and Broadcasting Policy*. London: HMSO.

Katz, E. (1971) Platforms and Windows: Broadcasting's Role

in Election Campaigns. *Journalism Quarterly* summer: 304–14. Also in D. McQuail (ed.) *Sociology of Mass Communications*. Harmondsworth: Penguin.

Katz, E. and Lazarsfeld, P. (1956) *Personal Influence: The Part Played by People in the flow of Mass Communications*. New York: Free Press.

King, J. and Stott, M. (eds) (1977) *Is This Your Life? Images of Women in the Media*. London: Virago.

Klapper, T. (1960) *The Effects of Mass Communication*. New York: Free Press.

Lazarsfeld, P., Berelson, B., and Gaudet, H. (1944) *The People's Choice*. New York: Columbia University Press.

McLuhan, M. (1964) *Understanding Media: The Extensions of Man*. New York: McGraw-Hill.

McNeill, P. (1985) *Research Methods*. London: Methuen.

McQuail, D. (ed.) (1972) *Sociology of Mass Communications*. Harmondsworth: Penguin.

—— (1977) The Influence and Effects of Mass Media. In J. Curran, M. Gurevitch, and J. Woollacott (eds) *Mass Communication and Society*. London: Edward Arnold.

McQuail, D., Blumler, D., and Brown, D. (1972) The Television Audience: A Revised Perspective. In D. McQuail (ed.) *Sociology of Mass Communications*. Harmondsworth: Penguin.

McRobbie, A. and Garber, J. (1976) Girls and Subcultures: An Exploration. In S. Hall and T. Jefferson (eds) *Resistance through Rituals*. London: Hutchinson.

Marsh, P., Rosser, E., and Harré, R. (1978) *The Rules of Disorder*. London: Routledge & Kegan Paul.

Morley, D. (1980) *The Nationwide Audience*. London: British Film Institute.

Morley, D. and Brunsdon, C. (1978) *Everyday Television: Nationwide*. London: British Film Institute.

Murdock, G. (1982) Large Corporations and the Control of the Communications Industries. In M. Gurevitch, T. Bennett, J. Curran, and J. Woollacott (eds) *Culture, Society and the Media*. London: Methuen.

Murdock, G. and McCron, R. (1979) The Television and Delinquency Debate. *Screen Education* 30 (spring).

Murphy, B. (1983) *The World Wired Up: Unscrambling the New Communication Puzzle*. London: Comedia.

132

Pahl, R. and Winkler, J. (1974) The Economic Elite. In P. Stanworth and A. Giddens (eds) *Elites and Power in British Society*. Cambridge: Cambridge University Press.

Palmer, J. (1973) Thrillers: The Deviant behind the Consensus. In I. Taylor and L. Taylor (eds) *Politics and Deviance*. Harmondsworth: Penguin.

Parkin, F. (1973) *Class Inequality and Political Order*. London: Paladin.

Pearce, F. (1981) The British Press and the 'Placing' of Homosexuality. In S. Cohen and J. Young (eds) *The Manufacture of News: Deviance, Social Problems and the Mass Media*. London: Constable.

Perkins, T. (1979) Rethinking Stereotypes. In M. Barrett, P. Corrigan, A. Kuhn, and J. Wolff (eds) *Ideology and Cultural Production*. London: Croom Helm.

Pickard, P.M. (1955) British Comics – An Appraisal. Pamphlet published by Comics Campaign Council. Cited in M. Barker (1984a) *A Haunt of Fears*. London: Pluto Press.

Raboy, M. (1983) Media and Politics in Socialist France. *Media, Culture and Society* 5 (3/4 July–October).

Reeve, A. and Stubbs, P. (1981) Racism and the Mass Media: Revising Old Perspectives. *Multiracial Education* 9 (2: spring).

Saussure, Ferdinand de (1974) *Course in General Linguistics*. London: Fontana.

Sieghart, P. (ed.) (1982) *Microchips with Everything: The Consequences of Information Technology*. London: Comedia.

Spender, D. (1980) *Man Made Language*. London: Routledge & Kegan Paul.

Streeter, T. (1983) Policy Discourse and Broadcast Practice. *Media, Culture and Society* 5 (3/4 July–October).

Trenaman, J. and McQuail, D. (1961) *Television and the Political Image*. London: Methuen.

Tuchman, G. (1981) The Symbolic Annihilation of Women by the Mass Media. In S. Cohen and J. Young (eds) *The Manufacture of News: Deviance, Social Problems and the Mass Media*. London: Constable.

Tunstall, J. (1983) *The Media in Britain*. London: Constable.

Wallington, P. (1984) Freedom of Speech. In P. Wallington (ed.) *Civil Liberties 1984*. Oxford: Martin Robertson.

Weber, M. (1964) *The Theory of Social and Economic Organization*. New York: Free Press.

Wertham, F. (1953) *The Seduction of the Innocent*. New York: Holt, Rinehart & Winston.

Westergaard, J. (1977) Power, Class, and the Media. In J. Curran, M. Gurevitch, and J. Woollacott (eds) *Mass Communication and Society*. London: Edward Arnold.

White, D.M. (1950) The Gatekeeper: A Case Study in the Selection of News. *Journalism Quarterly* 27: 383–90.

Wilkins, L. (1981) Information and the Definition of Deviance. In S. Cohen and J. Young (eds) *The Manufacture of News: Deviance, Social Problems and the Mass Media*. London: Constable.

Williams, R. (1965) *The Long Revolution*. Harmondsworth: Pelican.

Williamson, J. (1978) *Decoding Advertisements*. London: Marion Boyars.

Willis, P. (1978) *Profane Culture*. London: Routledge & Kegan Paul.

Young, J. (1971) *The Drugtakers: The Social Meanings of Drug Use*. London: MacGibbon & Kee.

Index

Marsh, P. 41
Marxist approaches 16, 28, 51–3, 55–7, 60–1, 91
mass communication 14–15
media: as industry 15; as scapegoat 21; 'commercial' model 30; 'critical' approach 51
media organizations 58–9; bureaucratic influences 95–7; growth in size 65–7; influence of advertisers 61–3; other commercial influences 68–9, 85
media research: content analysis 103–07; development 16–18 experimental 21–5; field 22, 25–7; methods 11; semantic differential 51, 107–08; semiology 15, 108–17; sponsorship 7, 20; uses and gratifications 29, 35–6, 124
media technology 10–11, 14, 59, 79, 83, 84–91; cable TV 79, 86–90; determinism 84–5; economic effects 79, 89; information technology 86; satellites 79, 86–90
Middleton, S. 40, 54–7
montage 115
moral entrepreneurs 6, 7, 24
moral panics 37–8, 40, 54–5
Morley, D. 50, 115, 125–27
mugging 56, 100
Murdock, G. 20–2, 25–7, 60, 68–9
Murphy, B. 102

National Union of Teachers 3, 6, 7
Nationwide 125–27
news: agencies 80, 93, 99; gatekeepers 92–3; manufacture 91–102;

primary and secondary definers 56, 96, 101; values 49, 94–9
Nias, D. 21–5

O'Sullivan, T. 117, 127
Official Secrets see state
opinion leaders 30–1
ownership of media 64–8

Pahl, R. 66
Palmer, J. 37
paradigm 110
Parkin, F. 126
Pearce, F. 47
Perkins, T. 44–5
Pickard, P. M. 5
police see state
preferred reading 117–18
Press: electronic newspaper 86; fourth estate 70; free press 62, 66, 69–71; growth of 62–9; radical press 62
primary definers see news
psychological approaches 9, 15, 21–5, 33, 43

Raboy, M. 80
race 25, 32–3, 44, 48, 56, 98
realism 111
Reeve, A. 50
Robins, D. 34
Rosser, E. 41
Ruge, M. 49, 95, 101

satellites see media technology
Saunders, D. 117
Saussure, F. de 111
Seaton, J. 16–17, 32, 62, 67, 72, 102
semantic differential see media research
semiology see media research
sensitization 39–40